USA TODAY

A GANNETT COMPANY

Lifeline
BIOGRAPHIES

RUSSELL SIMMONS
From Def Jam to *Super Rich*

by Carrie Golus

Twenty-First Century Books · Minneapolis

Twenty-First Century Books
A division of Lerner Publishing Group, Inc.
241 First Avenue North
Minneapolis, MN 55401 U.S.A.

Website address: www.lernerbooks.com

Library of Congress Cataloging-in-Publication Data

Golus, Carrie, 1969–
    Russell Simmons : from Def Jam to *Super Rich* / by Carrie Golus.
        p. cm. — (USA today lifeline biographies)
    Includes bibliographical references and index.
    ISBN 978-0-7613-8157-0 (lib. bdg. : alk. paper)
    1. Simmons, Russell—Juvenile literature. 2. Sound recording executives and producers—United States—Biography—Juvenile literature. 3. Def Jam Recordings—Juvenile literature. I. Title.
ML3930.S545G66 2012
782.421649092—dc22 [B]   2011018063

Manufactured in the United States of America
1 – PP – 12/31/11

![USA TODAY](A GANNETT COMPANY) **Lifeline** BIOGRAPHIES

INTRODUCTION

Hip-hop history: Russell Simmons oversees a recording session in a studio in New York in 1993. Simmons is an influential figure in the history of hip-hop music.

Godfather of Hip-Hop

The mid-1990s was "one of the saddest periods in hip-hop's history," Russell Simmons once declared. In September 1996, rapper Tupac Shakur was gunned down as he rode in a car in Las Vegas, Nevada. He was twenty-five years old. Less than a year later, in March 1997, rapper Biggie Smalls was shot and killed in a Los Angeles, California, parking lot. He was twenty-four. Once friends, Shakur and Smalls had

Feud: Tupac Shakur *(left)* and Biggie Smalls *(right)* were shot and killed within one year of each other during a time of rivalry between East Coast and West Coast rappers.

been sucked into a rivalry between East Coast and West Coast rappers.

Feuds had been a part of hip-hop since its beginnings in the 1970s. In the early days, hip-hop rivalries were usually good-natured. But the East Coast-West Coast feud was different. Rappers from each side wrote angry songs about each other. They made music videos showing their rivals being injured or killed. Shakur, representing the West Coast, and Smalls, representing the East Coast, both took part.

"I was with Biggie just ten minutes before he got shot," Simmons recalled in his 2001 autobiography, *Life and Def: Sex, Drugs, Money and God*. The two had shared a table at a party. Biggie, who was recovering from a leg injury, was walking with a cane. "When Tupac's 'California Love' came on, I'll never forget how Biggie held up his cane and bobbed it in the air to the beat. He loved that record, despite the fact that Tupac had attacked him so often in interviews and on record. That night he was happy, and all that mess didn't seem to concern him."

Advice: During the East-West feud, Simmons contacted Louis Farrakhan *(above)*. Farrakhan is the leader of the Nation of Islam and is respected among many African Americans.

Police had no actual proof that the unsolved shootings were connected to the East–West dispute. But Simmons, then thirty-nine, was still concerned. He did not want the killings to turn the rivalry into a full-scale bicoastal war.

As the founder of Def Jam, one of hip-hop's oldest record labels, Simmons had influence in the hip-hop world and elsewhere. After Smalls's death, Simmons contacted Louis Farrakhan, leader of the religious and social organization the Nation of Islam. Farrakhan was controversial. Over the years, he had made many antiwhite and anti-Semitic (anti-Jewish) statements. Nevertheless, he was a powerful leader in the African American community. Simmons helped arrange a meeting at Farrakhan's home in Chicago, Illinois.

Rappers and music executives from both coasts were invited. The guests listened to Farrakhan speak, had a meal together, and socialized. "That meeting, along with the shock of Tupac's and Biggie's deaths, cooled everybody off and helped squash the rhetoric [irresponsible public talk]," Simmons recalled.

Helping to end the East Coast-West Coast feud was a typical move for Simmons. As a native New Yorker whose record label was based in Manhattan, he could have easily been drawn into the war. But he had steered clear of the dispute. He had even collaborated on a few projects with Marion "Suge" Knight, head of the notorious West Coast label Death Row.

Although Simmons did not take a front seat in settling the dispute, he worked behind the scenes. He had connections to both sides of the rivalry and to Farrakhan. Like the dealmaker he is, Simmons put all the major players in a room together and then stepped aside while they worked it out.

Making the New Mainstream

Entrepreneur Russell Simmons defies easy description. A 1984 article in the business newspaper the *Wall Street Journal* labeled Simmons "the mogul of rap." Since then he's been called the godfather of hip-hop, a hip-hop impresario [promoter], and the CEO [chief executive officer]

On tour: Marion "Suge" Knight is the former head of Death Row Records. Simmons collaborated with Knight midway through the East-West feud.

IN F⦿CUS

East vs. West

The feud between East Coast and West Coast rappers began in the early 1990s. California hip-hop had been growing in popularity. Artists from both coasts boasted about who could sell the most albums. The rivalry took a dangerous turn in 1994, when Tupac Shakur was shot for the first time. The people who assaulted Shakur were never caught, but Shakur believed that Biggie Smalls and Sean Combs had set him up. In 1995 the feud worsened. At the *Source* Awards—a ceremony hosted by the popular hip-hop magazine the *Source*—Death Row Records founder Suge Knight insulted Combs while accepting an award. The pattern of insults and violence continued until the deaths of Shakur and Smalls.

of hip-hop. The online magazine *Salon* summed up his contributions this way: "Russell Simmons didn't invent rap, but he is, perhaps more than any other individual, responsible for the music's astonishing success."

When Simmons cofounded the Def Jam record label in 1984, some people—including many African American music executives—thought rap was a passing fad. Simmons was one of the few to realize that hip-hop music had staying power. He also believed that the influence of hip-hop culture would extend beyond the music industry. Those insights have made Simmons a powerful figure in the music world.

Simmons has often been compared to Berry Gordy Jr., founder of Motown Records. Motown, one of the first independent labels owned by an African American, released a string of hits in the 1960s and the 1970s. The label's artists included Smokey Robinson, Diana Ross and the Supremes, Marvin Gaye, the Jackson 5, and many more. But while Gordy wanted his black artists to appeal to a white audience, Simmons succeeded by taking the opposite approach. "I don't believe in catering to the so-called mainstream by altering your look or slang or music," he wrote in his autobiography. "I see hip-hop culture as the new American mainstream. We don't change for you; you adapt to us." Simmons has been able to market hip-hop to a wide audience without pushing away its original fans.

Simmons has also refused to compromise his own tastes to further his success. While his style has shifted over the years, sneakers (always sparkling clean) and baseball caps are staples—no matter how formal the occasion. "Russell was legendary," recalled Nelson George, author and one-time editor for music magazine *Billboard*. "He was the point man for rap, but he still wore his sneakers untied and refused to wear anything like adult clothing." Simmons's conversation is also famously littered with swear words, even in business meetings. In spite of—or perhaps because of—his refusal to conform to ideas of what a businessperson should be like, Simmons has created his own million-dollar hip-hop empire.

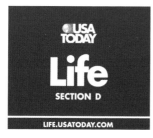

USA TODAY

Life

SECTION D

LIFE.USATODAY.COM

September 10, 1996

Was Shakur victim in rap industry rivalry?

From the Pages of
USA TODAY

As Tupac Shakur had his right lung removed Monday in Las Vegas, speculation in the music world was whether his wounding was part of a competition between East Coast and West Coast [hip-hop artists] to sell records and dominate the rap world. Shakur remained in critical condition Monday at University Medical Center after being shot several times in the chest Saturday when he and Marion "Suge" Knight, head of Death Row Records, were driving to a nightclub. L.A.-based Death Row, a label specializing in gangsta rap, boasts Shakur, Snoop Doggy Dogg, Hammer and others. They are rivals with Sean "Puffy" Combs, head of Manhattan's Bad Boy Entertainment, home of the Notorious B.I.G.

Shakur has said that a 1994 incident in which he got shot five times was a set-up. "Tupac really believes Biggie and them shot him," Ice-T says in the new *Vibe*. "If somebody thinks they shot them, it's on for life." Police said Monday they had no suspects and were getting no cooperation from Shakur's entourage.

While the East-West rivalry is an initial theory for the shooting, *Vibe* magazine editor in chief Alan Light says he "wouldn't be surprised if it didn't have anything to do with Tupac, but is more related to Suge. There have been up to three contracts on his life at any given moment. He's very public . . . about his gang affiliation. There are a lot of people with a lot of issues with him." Besides, Shakur was just in New York at the MTV video awards, and if this were a turf war, it's more likely something would have happened then, Light adds.

In the September issue of *The Source*, Knight says, "Ain't no East coast/West coast thang. That ain't it." But Combs, in the September *Vibe*, says, "I'm ready for it to come to a head, however it gotta go down . . . I just hope it can end quick and in a positive way, because it's gotten out of hand."

—Ann Oldenburg

Hometown: The Queensboro Bridge, pictured here in the 1970s, connects the New York City boroughs of Manhattan and Queens. Simmons grew up in Queens.

Childhood in Queens

Russell Simmons was born on October 4, 1957, in Queens, New York. His parents, Evelyn and Daniel Simmons, had met at Howard University in Washington, D.C. His mother had studied sociology and psychology at Howard. His father had studied history. Russell was the couple's second son. Their first child, Danny, was born a few years earlier. Another son, Joseph (Joey), was born in 1964.

The Simmons family lived in a two-bedroom house in a Queens neighborhood called Jamaica. Danny and Russell shared a bunk bed in a home filled with toys. Both parents worked, so the family depended on a housekeeper-babysitter who came to help out several days a week.

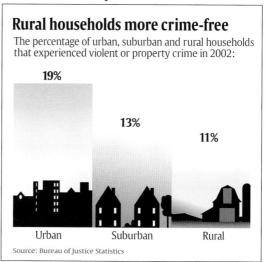

USA TODAY Snapshots®

Rural households more crime-free

The percentage of urban, suburban and rural households that experienced violent or property crime in 2002:

19%

13%

11%

Urban   Suburban   Rural

Source: Bureau of Justice Statistics

By Shannon Reilly and Julie Snider, USA TODAY, 2004

Queens is one of New York City's five boroughs (or districts), along with Manhattan, Brooklyn, the Bronx, and Staten Island. The Jamaica neighborhood's busy main street, Jamaica Avenue, had several department stores and an old-fashioned movie theater. One of Russell's earliest memories was walking with his parents under the street's elevated train tracks. But his neighborhood was somewhat rural too. Some of the neighbors kept chickens in their backyards. The children searched the nearby woods for snakes to take home as pets. Russell became known for his complete lack of fear around snakes.

Many of the African American parents in Jamaica had grown up in the southern United States. They had moved north in search of more opportunity. But Evelyn Simmons had grown up in Queens. She was the daughter of one of New York's first African American nurses. Evelyn worked as a preschool teacher for the New York City Parks Department. She was also an amateur painter.

Russell's father came from a very different background. He had grown up poor in Baltimore, Maryland. He was able to attend college

Family: Russell *(left)* attends a benefit with his brother Daniel Simmons *(right)* in 2010. Russell's older brother is a painter, a poet, and an activist.

only because he had served in the army, which paid his tuition bills. An administrator for New York's Board of Education, Daniel Simmons was well-read and worldly. But he never forgot where he came from, and he hated snobbery in any form.

Russell admired his father, who was popular in the community. Daniel was involved with several civil rights organizations in New York. Russell once witnessed his father lying down in front of a bulldozer to protest racial discrimination in the hiring of construction workers. His father's convictions made a deep impression on young Russell.

Like Evelyn, Daniel also had an interest in the arts. A stocky man with a deep, rich voice, he could recite lines from *Hamlet* and enjoyed writing poetry. "Even as a small child, I was aware of the creative energy they both radiated," Simmons recalled about his parents. "In the Simmons family... we are all creative, strong-willed, dynamic people."

Hollis

In 1965, when Russell was eight, the Simmons family moved to Hollis, a quiet, middle-class community in southeastern Queens. At the time, Hollis was about 10 percent white. But as more and more African American families moved in, most white families moved out. On the street where the Simmons family settled, just one white family

IN F☉CUS

Black Migration and White Flight

Throughout the first half of the twentieth century, African Americans moved away from the southern United States in large numbers. Events such as World War I (1914–1918) and the growth of automobile use created new jobs in industries such as manufacturing. Many African Americans moved to northern states in search of these jobs.

By the mid-1900s, African American populations had greatly increased in cities throughout the North. Large numbers of whites began moving to suburban areas outside of cities around the same time. The Civil Rights movement of the 1950s and the 1960s marked the end of laws that treated whites and non-whites unfairly or kept them separated in schools. People of many races protested these unfair laws. Even so, segregation continued unofficially in many neighborhoods throughout the United States. For instance, some

real estate agents led blacks looking for housing to areas that were largely black, rather than racially mixed. By the end of the twentieth century, the living areas of urban African Americans were nearly as segregated as the neighborhoods of African Americans a century earlier.

Civil rights: Protesters call for equal treatment during the March on Washington for Jobs and Freedom in 1963.

remained. That family soon joined the "white flight" too.

The Simmons's house was typical of Hollis. It had two floors and a small yard. Russell shared a room with Joey. People who could afford to move to Hollis came from Brooklyn, Harlem (in Manhattan), and other more established African American neighborhoods in New York. As the neighborhood's population changed from white to black, so did the neighborhood schools. Russell's parents arranged for him to go to integrated (racially mixed) schools in a nearby white area of Queens.

At mixed schools, Russell learned to deal with many different types of people. He came to believe that there were many superficial differences between the races. But on a deeper level, everyone wanted similar things out of life. "I could play baseball with the white boys and basketball with the black boys," he recalled, "and I saw kinship where others saw difference."

Drugs and Gangs

In the early 1970s, another significant shift occurred in Hollis. Like many African American neighborhoods in New York, Hollis was overrun by heroin. As the drug dealers moved in, the neighborhood became more dangerous.

Russell's parents were hardworking people who put their family first. Nonetheless, the culture of drugs was everywhere, and Danny and Russell got caught up in it. At first, Danny's drug of choice was LSD, or acid. Later, he became addicted to heroin. When his parents found out, they kicked him out of the house. Danny spent most of his teen years living with Evelyn's mother in Jamaica, Queens.

Meanwhile, Russell became a minor drug dealer. He sold marijuana on 205th Street, a drug-dealing strip two blocks from his house. He hid his supply of marijuana in the bushes in front of his family's home.

Once the police caught Russell and a friend smoking marijuana in public. The boys' pockets were full of bags of marijuana, which they meant to sell later. Russell was arrested and spent the night in jail. A judge put him on probation (supervision by a court officer) for a year and a half. Still, he did not stop selling drugs.

When he was sixteen years old, Russell was robbed by Red, a local criminal whose specialty was sticking up drug dealers. A few weeks later, Russell ran into Red again. This time Russell was with a group of other dealers. He and the

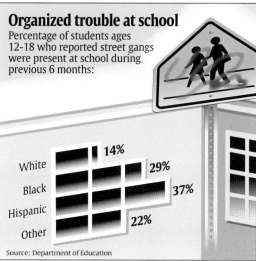

USA TODAY Snapshots®

Organized trouble at school

Percentage of students ages 12-18 who reported street gangs were present at school during previous 6 months:

White 14%
Black 29%
Hispanic 37%
Other 22%

Source: Department of Education

By David Stuckey and Frank Pompa, USA TODAY, 2006

others chased Red down and cornered him in a nearby backyard. Then someone handed Russell a gun.

Russell took the weapon, aimed, fired, and missed. It was the first and the last time he would ever shoot a gun at another human being. Afterward, he boasted to his friends that he would not miss the next time. But as he later recalled, he knew that missing Red was the luckiest thing that had ever happened to him.

Russell also got caught up in another scourge of 1970s New York—street gangs. As a teenager, he joined a local gang called the Seven Immortals, becoming a warlord in the gang's seventeenth division. Showing an early talent for salesmanship, Russell helped recruit new members, most of them between the ages of fourteen and sixteen.

With members so young, the Seven Immortals was not a particularly tough gang. They got into fights and committed petty crimes, but they did not carry guns. On one occasion, Russell and his friends found out just how un-tough they were. They made a day trip to Coney Island, a beach and park area in Brooklyn. Some members of the Black

Spades gang were also there. The typical Black Spades member was thirty years old and had spent time in prison. When the Black Spades heard the Seven Immortals were at Coney Island, they came looking for the young gang.

At the time, gang members wore their jean jackets inside out and drew the gang's markings on the back. When Russell heard that the Black Spades were looking for the Seven Immortals, he set aside group loyalty in favor of self-preservation. "I threw [my gang jacket] in the garbage," Russell recalled later. "We were just trying to figure out how to get back to Queens." Terrified, he and his friends split up and headed home.

Russell eventually dropped out of gang life after one of the Seven Immortals was murdered by another rival gang, the Seven Crowns. "Gang membership, then and now, provides a sense of family for a lot of people," he recalled. "I guess it hit me that I already had a strong family, so why was I risking my safety like this?"

Fake Drugs

Daniel Simmons worried that his middle son's involvement in drugs and gangs would eventually land him in prison. When Russell was a senior in high school, his father found him a job. He hoped work would keep Russell busy and out of trouble. Russell was hired to serve up frothy fruit drinks at an Orange Julius stand in Greenwich Village, a neighborhood in Manhattan. Greenwich Village was a completely different world from Hollis. It was racially mixed and home to a vibrant community of artists.

While Russell's job did keep him busy, it didn't entirely keep him out of trouble. Russell soon discovered that coca leaf incense was being sold under the counter of the store next to Orange Julius. Coca leaf incense was a perfectly legal product. But when it was chopped up and packaged in foil, it looked like cocaine. Because the caffeine in it gave users a small high, most customers thought they had purchased real cocaine. Dealers sold the incense under the counter to make it seem

The Village: When Russell was a senior in high school, he worked in Greenwich Village, pictured here in 1968. Greenwich Village is a racially mixed, artistic neighborhood in Manhattan.

like a real drug sale. Russell started selling coca leaf incense himself.

Russell earned a lot more money on the coca leaf incense scam than he earned at Orange Julius. And the one time he was arrested, he had to be released, because he wasn't breaking the law. He never even had any complaints from dissatisfied customers.

Music and Fashion

With so much extra spending money, Russell developed a new and lasting obsession—fashion. He liked to buy alligator- and lizard-skin shoes, sharkskin (a smooth fabric) pants, and Kangol caps—the style of trendy, upscale clothing that was popular among young, urban black men at the time. At one point, he had a preference for a particular type of silk-and-wool pants that cost thirty-two dollars. In his

During World War II (1939–1945), members of the British armed forces wore berets made by the company Kangol. The company's hats landed on a new set of heads during the 1980s, as Kangol berets and caps became staples of hip-hop fashion.

autobiography, Simmons noted that he could have bought a similar pair of pants for just seven dollars—but he didn't.

Russell's obsession wasn't just about what clothes cost but how exclusive they were. In the mid-1970s, the sneaker to have was a make of Keds called 69ers. At one point, Keds stopped manufacturing them, which just made Russell want them more. He traveled to shoe outlets all over the city just to track down the specific sneaker he wanted.

Meanwhile, Russell developed a second, equally lasting obsession—music. In particular, he loved rhythm and blues, or R & B. Among his early favorites were groups such as the Delfonics, the Dells, the Dramatics, the Moments, the Detroit Emeralds, Blue Magic, and Black Ivory. "The music I liked was very ghetto and gritty," he recalled. "It was the stuff that didn't really cross over much [appeal to whites], but spoke to a roots black experience."At a time when it was easier for underage kids to get into dance clubs, the teenage Russell liked to hang out at the Casablanca Club in Queens or Nell Gwyn's in Manhattan.

Russell had never been particularly interested in music before, other than loving Elvis Presley movies as a child. But in high school, it became his life. "He would just talk me to death about music," his brother Danny recalled. "He would not shut up about music. Russell was so singularly driven about this music thing that it got on my nerves. I'm like, 'Can't you talk about anything else?' And his answer was 'No. There's nothing else to talk about.'"

IN FOCUS

The Roots of R & B

Jerry Wexler, a writer for *Billboard* magazine, first coined the term *rhythm and blues* in the late 1940s. In 1949 *Billboard* officially adopted the term as the name for its chart of hits in African American popular music. R & B itself took shape in the 1930s. African American musicians began making music that took elements from earlier forms such as blues and jazz. Musicians such as Louis Jordan, Cab Calloway, and Count Basie wrote bluesy songs with upbeat, danceable rhythms. Although the guitar had been an important feature of blues music, it was not as central in many R & B groups.

Rock and roll emerged as a popular form of music alongside R & B in the 1950s. The difference between R & B and rock and roll was not always clear. Artists such as Little Richard and Ray Charles were known sometimes as R & B artists and sometimes as rock artists.

In the 1960s, the term *soul* also gained popularity. African American soul singers such as Sam Cooke and Aretha Franklin made music that was similar to earlier R & B but also easy to distinguish from the rock music made by mostly white performers. Soul replaced rhythm and blues as the name of *Billboard*'s black pop chart in 1969. Since the 1960s, people have often used *soul* and *R & B* interchangeably.

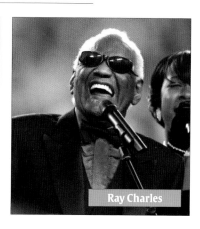

Ray Charles

Sam Cooke

Aretha Franklin

CCNY: Simmons attended the City College of New York (*above*) in Harlem. During college, Simmons and his friends attended early hip-hop shows in Harlem clubs.

Running the Track

In 1975 Simmons began his freshman year at the City College of New York (CCNY) in Harlem. To save money, he lived with his parents and commuted to Harlem from Queens.

Like his mother and his older brother, Simmons majored in sociology. But from the beginning, academic work was never really his focus. Instead, Simmons spent most afternoons in the CCNY student lounge, hanging out with a group of friends who enjoyed music and partying as much as he did.

As a high school senior, Simmons had developed the habit of taking LSD every Friday afternoon. This powerful drug causes users to have visions and feel intense emotions. As a college student, he discovered a new drug—PCP, or angel dust. "I loved getting 'dusty,'" Simmons recalled. "It made me happy." (During college, he acquired the nickname Rush, but he has denied the name is a reference to the "rush" a user gets from taking drugs.)

Simmons would begin a typical Friday night by smoking PCP and hanging out in the student lounge. When it got late enough, he and his friends would head to one of the nearby Harlem clubs that catered to a young, hip audience, such as Charles' Gallery on 125th Street.

Harlem clubs popular with older African American audiences usually featured live musical acts. But at Charles' Gallery, disc jockeys (DJs) spun records instead. One night in 1977, the club's lineup also included a master of ceremonies (MC) billed as the "world famous" Eddie Cheeba.

Like many of the earliest MCs, Cheeba rapped over the instrumental parts of existing records. His performance was a mix of chants to hype up the crowd (along the lines of "Somebody, anybody, everybody scream!") and rhymes about how cool he was. Many of the people in the audience had seen Cheeba before, and they rapped right along with him.

"It wasn't a sophisticated rhyme flow by current standards," Simmons recalled. "But hearing Cheeba in '77 made me feel I'd just witnessed the invention of the wheel." During the performance, Simmons realized that he somehow wanted to make hip-hop his career.

The obvious path would be to try to be a DJ or an MC himself. But Simmons knew that his talents didn't lie in this area. Instead, he decided to get into the business side. He would take the salesmanship he had developed as a minor drug dealer—and as a fake-drug dealer—and start a career in hip-hop music.

IN F⊙CUS

Hip-Hop vs. Rap

Hip-hop music typically features spoken rhyming lyrics, delivered over an instrumental track. "Samples," or short segments taken from other songs, are a common part of hip-hop songs. The terms *hip-hop* and *rap* are sometimes used interchangeably. However, *rap* refers to the act of delivering rhymes (rapping). *Hip-hop* refers to the culture surrounding this form of music in addition to the music itself.

The identity of the first rapper, like that of the first rock and roller, is unclear. Some argue it was Kool Herc, a Jamaican who started throwing block parties in the Bronx in 1973. Others trace hip-hop back to African American spoken-word poets such as Gil Scott-Heron. By the late 1970s, hip-hop music was thriving in the Bronx and in Harlem. Rappers and DJs were only part of the hip-hop scene. Other important aspects in the early days were graffiti and break dancing, a style of street dance that most famously involves spinning on your back or head.

The start: Kool Herc, pictured here in 2006, is thought to be one of the first rappers.

"It was such a good time for hip-hop culture," Simmons recalled later. At the time, part of the excitement of hip-hop was that it had to be experienced live, because hip-hop records didn't exist yet. To hear the music, fans had to go to the clubs, street parties, or parks where DJs and MCs put on a show. "They were *performing* artists," Simmons said. "They weren't rappers that make records, they didn't make songs. They made people happy."

Party Promoter

During his freshman year, Simmons had met a group of fellow students who were also aspiring party promoters. The group, which called itself the Force, gave parties at various Harlem clubs such as Charles' Gallery and Small's Paradise. Simmons decided he would try the same thing.

Simmons knew the competition in Harlem would be tough. He organized some parties there, including a regular night called "Terrible Tuesdays" at Small's. But he soon turned to his home turf, Queens. His first parties featured Curtis Walker, a Force member who was also a DJ and a rapper. Like many early hip-hop artists, Walker was a solo performer. He spun records and rapped at the same time, without the assistance of a DJ.

Simmons decided Walker needed a catchy name. They settled on Kurtis Blow. *Blow* is a slang term for the drug cocaine. The name referred to Walker's selling of coca leaf incense. The Blow nickname was also an attempt to copy the more established rapper Eddie Cheeba, whose last name was a slang term for marijuana. Simmons billed Blow as Queens' #1 rapper even though Blow had grown up in Harlem.

At the time, hip-hop was completely underground. Other kinds of

"Queens' #1 rapper": Kurtis Blow performs onstage in 1986. Blow spun records and rapped at some of Simmons parties in Queens, New York.

music were promoted through newspapers, TV, and radio. But hip-hop party promotion was strictly street-level. Simmons stuck flyers announcing his parties on lampposts and put up stickers in subways. It was technically illegal, but the city's ordinances against flyers and graffiti were rarely enforced. Simmons also relied on one legal method of promotion: word of mouth.

Calling himself Rush Productions, Simmons soon began booking shows that featured Blow and DJ Grandmaster Flash. Simmons's breakthrough success was a 1977 party at the Hotel Diplomat in Manhattan's Times Square. He booked Flash and Blow to perform. Two thousand hip-hop fans showed up. Simmons wasn't making big money yet, but a career in hip-hop suddenly seemed possible. It was, as he noted later, a much less stressful job than selling drugs.

At times, however, hip-hop promoting could be almost as dangerous. One night a number of fights broke out at the Hotel Diplomat. Simmons and Blow ended up hiding out in the Diplomat's bulletproof box office. Another incident occurred outside Fantasia, a club in a rough area of Queens. A group of kids started shooting at Simmons as he left the club at the end of the night. Simmons managed to escape by crawling under a car, still holding all the money he had made.

Simmons had already been a lackluster college student, but his new interest in party promotion marked the end to his academic career. "I actually did more schoolwork while selling drugs," he recalled. In his senior year, with just a few classes to go before graduation, he dropped out of college.

Simmons's father, who had fought hard to become a member of the middle class, was distraught. Daniel was convinced that the only way for an African American man to achieve success was to get a college degree and land a steady job. He saw party promotion as a hobby, not a career.

Evelyn Simmons was more open to her son's career choices, even if they led him down a less secure path. She believed in him, even when his shows lost money again and again.

IN FOCUS

Grandmaster Flash

Grandmaster Flash (Joseph Saddler) was already a hip-hop legend by the time he started performing with Kurtis Blow. Flash was one of the first hip-hop artists to "scratch" records during performances—running a vinyl record backward and forward on a turntable while it is playing. The scrape of a turntable's needle against a record became one of the most recognizable features of hip-hop music.

Flash has done his most well-known work with a group of rapping MCs known as the Furious Five. The group formed in New York's South Bronx in the mid-1970s. They released their first record, "Superrappin'," in 1979. The group soon gained fame with socially conscious songs such as "The Message" and "White Lines." Grandmaster Flash and the Furious Five split up in 1984 over business disputes, but they later reunited for a new album and tour. In 2007 they became the first hip-hop group to enter the Rock and Roll Hall of Fame.

Legend: Grandmaster Flash spins records in the 1980s. He was one of the first artists to scratch records while DJing.

At one point early in his career, Simmons booked DJ Hollywood, one of the biggest draws of the time, to do a show. But before the DJ Hollywood party could take place, Simmons lost all his savings on an unsuccessful Harlem party. With no money to make flyers or rent the club, he was going to have to cancel the Hollywood show.

Simmons's father was unsympathetic and told him it was time to go back to school. But his mother went into the house and returned with $2,000 in cash—her personal savings. "That act of love and faith," Simmons recalled, "which is what kept me in business at a key time, is my favorite memory of her."

"Christmas Rappin'"

By 1978 the Rush Productions flyers and subway stickers had caught the attention of Robert "Rocky" Ford, a writer for *Billboard*. Ford was curious about who was behind the promotions. One day he noticed Simmons's younger brother, Joey, hanging posters in Queens and gave him a business card. Russell called the next day. Soon afterward, Ford included him in an article on up-and-coming African American club owners and promoters. A few months later, Simmons helped Ford arrange interviews with rappers for an article on hip-hop—the first national story on the new genre.

With his party promotion career going well, Simmons wanted to take the next step. He wanted to produce hip-hop records. A record producer has an important, behind-the-scenes job. The producer coaches the performing artists and supervises the mixing and mastering of the recording. In some ways, a music producer's job is similar to that of a film director, who oversees and shapes the final creative product.

Simmons ended up working with Ford and another *Billboard* staffer, J. B. Moore, on a Kurtis Blow single called "Christmas Rappin'." Though it was his first time in the studio, Simmons took his role as coproducer seriously. He made suggestions about all aspects of the song—the lyrics, the melody, and the beat. The single was complete in the fall of 1979. Simmons then opened an artist-management company, Rush Management. Kurtis Blow was his first client.

As a *Billboard* writer, Ford had many contacts in the music industry, especially among African American executives. Rush Management tried to use Ford's contacts to get Blow a record deal. But the group

Rhyme of the boogie: The Sugar Hill Gang performs in the 1970s. Their song "Rapper's Delight" was the first hip-hop song to hit the Top 40.

found the music executives to be completely deaf to hip-hop. Black executives were usually older than hip-hop musicians and fans. They didn't care for the gritty music made by youngsters from the ghetto.

Simmons and the others had hoped that hip-hop was beginning to gain mainstream recognition. The Sugar Hill Gang's "Rapper's Delight," one of the earliest recorded hip-hop songs, had been released in 1979. The single was released by Sugar Hill Records, a small label in Englewood, New Jersey. "Rapper's Delight" went multiplatinum, selling more than two million copies. It became the first hip-hop song to hit the Top 40. But the record executives' view was that "Rapper's Delight" had been a fluke.

Undiscouraged, Simmons and the others dreamed up a plan to trick PolyGram into signing Blow. PolyGram was a major recording label already known for R & B and dance music. With artists such as Kool & the Gang, the Gap Band, and Parliament, PolyGram made sense as a possible home for Blow too.

Simmons made sample recordings of "Christmas Rappin'" and gave them out for free to clubs all over the city. DJs and clubbers loved the song. When stores wanted to carry it, Simmons told buyers they could order it through PolyGram. As the orders started rolling in for a record it didn't own yet, suddenly PolyGram became very interested.

Eventually Simmons helped Blow sign with Mercury Records, a division of PolyGram. Blow became the first rapper to sign with a major label. And in December 1979, "Christmas Rappin'" became the first hip-hop record released by a "major." The day the record came out, Simmons began "running the track," his term for obsessive promotion. "Christmas Rappin'" eventually went gold, meaning it sold five hundred thousand copies. The achievement was due as much to Simmons's tireless salesmanship as to Blow's artistry.

 "Christmas Rappin'" wasn't the last great hip-hop holiday song. In 1987 Run-D.M.C. released "Christmas in Hollis" as part of a benefit album for the Special Olympics.

Getting Paid

Based on the success of that one single, Simmons and Blow launched a concert tour. For the first half of 1980, they toured the whole country. Surprisingly, although "Christmas Rappin'" was a seasonal song, that didn't stop radio stations and clubs from playing it. Six months after Christmas had passed, Simmons and Blow were still touring places such as South Carolina, where fans had just discovered the song.

Simmons also traveled with Blow to Amsterdam, the Netherlands. It was his first trip abroad and his second on an airplane. When he stepped off the plane in Amsterdam, he found people addressing him as Mr. Simmons. The small gesture of respect meant an enormous amount to a college dropout from Queens. "That was the best payment," he recalled. "It reminded me that I deserved it, that I was doing something worthwhile. I haven't gotten anything better than that since."

With his share of the money from "Christmas Rappin'," Simmons was finally able to move out of his parents' house. He bought a house in Bedford-Stuyvesant, a neighborhood in Brooklyn. He and his girlfriend, Paulette Mims, moved in. The two were longtime friends from Hollis. They had started dating around the time Simmons went to college. Mims, who was still in high school when they first got together, was in the girls' division of the Seven Immortals.

As Simmons's career took off, he became less and less interested in a committed relationship. Soon after he bought the house, he moved out and left it to Mims. The breakup marked "the beginning of a very busy, wandering, ultra-decadent period," Simmons recalled—a period of excess in nearly every area of his life.

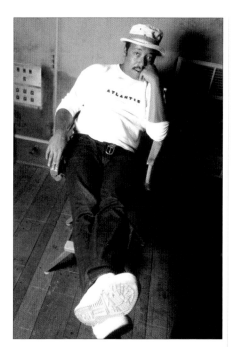

Starting to boom: In the early 1980s, Simmons's career was taking off and he opened his first office.

Rush Management

By 1982, when Simmons was twenty-five, his career had truly taken off. Blow had a second gold single, "The Breaks." Rush Management was managing the careers of ten artists. And Simmons opened his first office, a tiny space at 1133 Broadway in Manhattan. To keep costs down, he had just one employee, a secretary. The office had one piece of equipment, an ancient electric typewriter.

At the time, Simmons was one of the few professional managers who handled hip-hop acts. He certainly knew about hip-hop, but artist management was something he had to figure out on the job.

Simmons quickly realized that touring with hip-hop artists was much easier than with R & B acts. More traditional musical groups had more musicians, a lot of equipment, and roadies (road crew technicians) to help haul it all. A performer like Blow needed only a DJ and a road manager. His equipment setup was as spare as Rush's office. And because there were so few support personnel to pay, hip-hop performers—and their managers—made more money per person than traditional musical groups.

Soon Simmons increased his profits even more. Because Blow's act was so easily portable, Simmons could schedule several performances for him on the same day. Blow once performed in three different arenas in three states on one day: Birmingham, Alabama; Greensboro, North Carolina; and Augusta, Georgia.

Many times, Blow was a supporting act for traditional R & B artists. He was often the first hip-hop performer the audience had ever seen. While Simmons was helping set up the turntables, he sometimes heard audience members grumbling that they paid money to see a live band, not a DJ. But almost without exception, the audience was dancing by the end of the set.

Run-D.M.C.

At the time Simmons was touring with Kurtis Blow, Joey Simmons was beginning to show some musical talent. Joey had earned the nickname Run for his habit of running at the mouth, or talking a lot. Run had started taking drum lessons when he was ten. By twelve he had moved on to turntables. By thirteen he was DJing for Kurtis Blow. He performed as DJ Run Love, the son of Kurtis Blow, or DJ Run, his disco son. When he broke his arm, Run even learned to DJ with one arm.

Blow later got a different DJ. But Run continued making music with some childhood friends, Darryl McDaniels (D.M.C.) and Jason Mizell

MC rhymes: Russell managed his brother's rap group, Run-D.M.C. *From left:* Darryl McDaniels (D.M.C.), Jason Mizell (Jam Master Jay), and Joey Simmons (Run).

(Jam Master Jay). When the trio was unable to come up with a group name, Simmons suggested Run-D.M.C. None of them particularly liked it, but they couldn't think of anything better.

When Run was a senior in high school, Simmons booked some studio time for Run-D.M.C. With his younger brother's group, Simmons had the chance to produce a record that really sounded the way he wanted it to—like the music he heard on the street, with very little R & B influence. The result was the 12-inch (30-centimeter) record "It's Like That." The record's flip side was "Sucker MC's."

Simmons was proud of both songs, which had a stripped-down sound different from any other records at the time. But he was particularly proud of "Sucker MC's." Simmons had come up with the drumbeat for the song, which has been sampled on other records many times since.

June 8, 1988

Run-D.M.C. fight their bad rap

<u>From the Pages of</u>
<u>USA TODAY</u>

Even being the leader of the USA's top rap group can't quell this worry. Run of Run-D.M.C.—a.k.a. Joe Simmons—has heard he may have contracted a food parasite from an overseas visit. "Should've gotten checked out, man," says DJ Jam Master Jay (Jason Mizell). "Told you to see a doctor," says the bespectacled D.M.C. (Darryl McDaniels). "Stop it," Run says, rubbing his stomach. "I don't want to talk about it anymore."

This guy doesn't sound *Tougher Than Leather*—the title of their new album [and] their movie, due in August. Behind those gold chains and no-nonsense street garb are three affable 23-year-olds, as frightened of food parasites as of guns. These self-titled "kings of rap" reek of family values, having grown up in middle-class Hollis, in Queens, N.Y. Run and Jay still live there with their girlfriends. Run has two daughters (4 years old and 7 months); Jay has a 2-year-old son. D.M.C. lives with his folks in nearby Long Island City.

There were no instruments and no melody—only an electronic beat and a lot of yelling. "Because of the way it sounded and the impact it had on how people heard rap records," Simmons wrote in his autobiography, "I believe co-producing 'Sucker MC's' is the single most creative thing I've ever done."

Once again, Simmons approached African American executives at major labels. Once again, he found the doors were closed. Finally, he managed to get Run-D.M.C. signed with Profile Records, a small, white-owned hip-hop label in New York. Profile released "It's Like That" in the spring of 1983. The same year, Simmons added Run-D.M.C.

This group was the first rap act to earn a gold album (500,000 copies sold, 1984's *Run-D.M.C.*), first to earn a platinum (million-selling) and triple-platinum album (1986's *Raising Hell*) and first to have a top-five pop single, "Walk This Way."

"We just gotta let the (public) know that we are not negative people," Jay says. That hasn't been easy since that Long Beach, Calif., show in '86 where gang violence left 40 hurt. Since then, parents have called them a bad influence. Jay shakes his head: "We have to try to turn that around as much as possible."

During their 57-city *Run's House World Tour*, they're letting groups use their concert areas to promote summer jobs for youths and voter registration. Their new, fourth LP discusses an absentee father ("Papa Crazy") and the dangers of crack ("I'm Not Going Like That"). The music is just as tough as Run-D.M.C's attire—"Mary, Mary" sizzles with a guitar solo to rival Van Halen.

"Rap started in the street, and the street is tough," says D.M.C. "Therefore our music, as a whole, is tough. That's how we came up with the title." The title may have been the easiest part—it took the trio two years to get the album out. "We were doing so many other things," Run says. "And when we were ready to drop an album, we had trouble with our record company."

The group and the label are friends again (a new contract calls for 10 albums), and the movie's finally finished. "It's an adventure, a drama and it's funny," D.M.C. says. "We save somebody's honor and end up heroes." To millions of record-buyers, they already are.

—James T. Jones IV

to Rush Management's growing list of artists.

In 1984 Run-D.M.C. released its self-titled first album. *Run-D.M.C.* became the first rap album to be certified gold. Simmons helped mold Run-D.M.C. into a marketable group. Years later, Run credited his brother with having the vision to see a groundbreaking rap crew where others saw only three black teenagers who didn't play instruments. "Without Russell, knowing all this street stuff, with no business sense, probably [hip-hop music] would have stayed in Hollis," Run recalled. "He took the beat from the street and put it on TV."

Record promoter: Russell works in his office in 1988. He was rarely seen without a hat on his head and a phone in his hand.

Def Jam

By 1984 Simmons had the largest management company in the hip-hop world. Rush Management oversaw the careers of Kurtis Blow, Whodini, the Fearless Four, and a long list of up-and-coming performers. Simmons split time between managing artists and producing records.

Both Simmons and hip-hop were beginning to achieve a small measure of recognition in the wider culture. Simmons was even featured in an article in the *Wall Street Journal*, which called him the most powerful man in hip-hop. "Rap wasn't [much]," at the time, Simmons later recalled, "but I was the mogul anyway."

Partying was part of the job description. One night at a club, Simmons ran into DJ Jazzy Jay, who—along with T La Rock—had recently released a single Simmons loved, "It's Yours." Jazzy Jay asked Simmons if he wanted to meet the record's producer, who was also in the club that night. To Simmons's amazement, it turned out to be Rick Rubin, a "stocky, long-haired Long Island white kid."

Rubin was a film and video student at New York University (NYU). The first record he had released was an EP (or "extended-play" release—longer than a single but shorter than an album) of his own band, Hose, in 1982. Hose's innovative music, known as art punk or artcore, has been called a forerunner to alternative rock. Rubin played guitar.

Hose's EP was distributed by the independent record label 99 Records. But Rubin also put his own logo on it—Def Jam Recordings, along with his dorm room address. "It's Yours" was distributed by Streetwise records, but it also carried the Def Jam logo.

When Simmons and Rubin started talking, they realized that they had much more in common than their backgrounds would suggest. They liked the same sort of hip-hop music—hard beats, aggressive vocals, and little if any melody. They also hated the same sort of music—the soft R & B then being played on the radio. And they shared a similar sense of humor and a passion for networking while nightclubbing. The two began to spend a lot of time together, hanging out in clubs or in Rubin's dorm room.

Rubin told Simmons that Run-D.M.C.'s "Rock Box"—a song that Simmons had coproduced—had inspired him to get into making hip-hop records. "There weren't a lot of great rap records in those days," Rubin recalled about Simmons, "but any ones that were good, his name was on."

Def Jam

Rubin had the idea of making Def Jam into a full-fledged record company, not just a logo and a dorm room address. He had received a

July 7, 2006

Rick Rubin, music's rock

From the Pages of
USA TODAY
Artistic inspiration drives this edgy, prolific producer, who has a new slew of hits and more music on the way. He has a boyish laugh and a mountain-man burliness, a taste for demonic speed-metal and angelic doo-wop harmonies. Rick Rubin may be as impossible to pigeonhole as the starry and swollen catalog of music he has produced.

Declared by *Rolling Stone* the most successful producer in any genre, Rubin is a studio savant whose highly sought services launch trends and resuscitate icons. He's having a banner year as the knob-twirler behind a trio of hot albums. The Red Hot Chili Peppers' *Stadium Arcadium* bowed at No. 1 in May, followed two weeks later by the chart-topping debut of the Dixie Chicks' *Taking the Long Way*. This week, Johnny Cash's posthumous *American V: A Hundred Highways*, the fifth collaboration between Rubin and the country giant, hit shelves.

Highways, recorded in the last months of Cash's life, is cause for bittersweet celebration. Their collaboration represents another incongruity. Rubin initially struck Cash as a hobo. As their friendship deepened, they took daily communion together. They met in 1993, when Cash was at a low ebb creatively. "I thought it would be a challenge to find a true legend who wasn't doing his best and see if we could change that," Rubin says. "Johnny was the first person I thought of, someone without peer, still capable of good work."

Their first outing, 1994's *American Recordings*, reignited [Cash's] career and drew young fans. Arguably the best in the American series, *Highways* and its sly wisdom,

demo tape (sample recording) from a sixteen-year-old aspiring rapper named James Todd Smith III. Smith was nicknamed LL Cool J, short for "Ladies Love Cool James." Rubin wanted LL Cool J to be the first artist Def Jam signed as a real record company.

By this point, Rubin had already released four independent records vulnerability and steely sense of acceptance defy conventional wisdom in the music industry, where artists normally peak early and fade. "It shows he was a true, honest artist and a great legendary hero from beginning to end," Rubin says.

Cash is the warmest chapter in Rubin's career, launched in 1984 when the Long Island native and Russell Simmons co-founded the Def Jam label, "a fun hobby that ended up being my job." A rap fanatic, Rubin soaked up "aggressive sounds and outlaw music" after growing up on heavy metal, punk, James Brown, The Beatles, Led Zeppelin, oldies radio and doo-wop. As a producer, he made an immediate impact, playing a key role in rap's rise with such pivotal works as LL Cool J's *Radio*, the Beastie Boys' *Licensed to Ill* and Public Enemy's *Yo! Bum Rush the Show*. In the early '90s, he left Def Jam and founded the rock-freighted Def American. In 1991, he delivered the Peppers' breakthrough *Blood Sugar Sex Magik* plus parental nightmares by Slayer and [Andrew] Dice [Clay].

Zen producer: Rick Rubin posing in 1986. *Rolling Stone* has called Rubin the most successful producer in music.

Why does this meditating vegan (someone who consumes no meat, dairy, or other animal products) delight in music's wicked fringes? "I like things that are unique and extreme," he says. Steeped in the edgier realms of metal and rap, Rubin retained his Zen vibe. He never tried drugs. "When I was young, I was into magic [tricks]. Kids I knew did drugs or got drunk out of boredom. I didn't want to give up my time."

Nominated three times for a Grammy producer of the year award, [Rubin] isn't driven by hits or honors. It's the journey. His role is "to inspire and challenge artists to do their best work, and to do it for the sake of the work as opposed to the ends," Rubin says. "I try to erase all the restrictions that I've seen impede great art over and over. If the album is great, everything else will follow."

—Edna Gundersen

on his own. But he knew that for Def Jam to succeed financially, he needed Simmons's connections, as well as his experience with major labels, tours, and artist management.

When Rubin played LL Cool J's tape for Simmons, Simmons loved it. But he wasn't sure he wanted to start his own record company. Finally,

Rubin promised to make all the records and run the label out of his dorm room. All he asked from Simmons was that he be a partner. Simmons agreed.

In 1984 Simmons and Rubin signed a deal that made them equal partners in Def Jam. Rubin's wealthy parents put in $5,000, Simmons another $1,000. With that tiny investment, the label was launched. "We started the record company and nobody could tell us what to do," Simmons recalled. "It was our own little independent company."

Def Jam's first release was LL Cool J's 1984 single "I Need

Cool James: LL Cool J attends the American Music Awards in 1987. His single "I Need a Beat" was Def Jam's first release.

a Beat." Its second was "Rock Hard" by the Beastie Boys, one of the first all-white hip-hop groups. "Rock Hard" was an early example of rap-rock fusion, sampling AC/DC's "Back in Black." Both records were successes. By 1985 Def Jam had sold almost five hundred thousand records.

Indie Meets Major

Soon after founding Def Jam, Simmons and Rubin met with several major label executives. They hoped to find a major label that would distribute Def Jam's records. Some of the executives had no idea what to make of hip-hop music. Simmons recalled one meeting at Warner Brothers where he played LL Cool J's "I Need a Beat" for a group of executives. "It was like they were hearing music from another planet," Simmons remembered. "I wasn't offended—it was funny."

IN F⊙CUS

The Hip-Hop–Punk Rock Connection

Hip-hop and punk rock don't sound as if they have much in common. Punk is known for blaring guitars and screamed melodies, sounds rarely associated with hip-hop. However, some of Def Jam's most famous faces came from a punk music background.

Rick Rubin first learned to record music while a member of the art-punk band Hose. Hose's sound was sludgier and slower than that of many other punk bands. But like other members of New York's 1980s punk scene, Hose worked to make music that was wild and original. Rubin brought this spirit to his work with hip-hop artists. Playing with other musicians also made it clear to guitarist Rubin that bass and drums give a song its basic shape.

The Beastie Boys originally played an extremely fast, aggressive form of punk known as hardcore. After a while, the Beasties put down their instruments and turned to rapping—but they kept their punk rock attitude. Their music's rebellious sense of humor helped make Mike D (Mike Diamond), MCA (Adam Yauch), and Ad-Rock (Adam Horovitz) some of Def Jam's best-selling artists and the first successful white rappers.

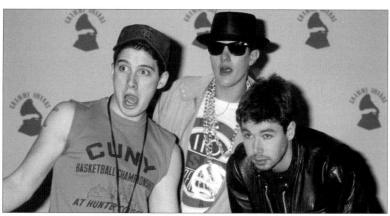

Punk rock hip-hop: The Beastie Boys attend the Grammy Awards in 1987. *From left:* Ad-Rock (Adam Horovitz), Mike D (Mike Diamond), and MCA (Adam Yauch). The Beastie Boys were one of the first white hip-hop groups and were on the Def Jam label.

The executives at Columbia had a similar reaction when Simmons and the others made a presentation. "It was just this unveiling of this subculture that was received with these big smiles and laughs, and headshaking," one young Columbia staffer recalled. "Like, 'Oh my God, there's this whole other world out there.'" At the time, Columbia's African American music roster featured fairly traditional acts. But the label had a history of taking chances on artists who pushed boundaries and became huge stars—such as Bob Dylan in 1962 and the Clash in 1977.

Simmons charmed Columbia's executives. And he had extra credibility because he managed Run-D.M.C., which by then had become the country's number one rap group.

Def Jam signed a distribution agreement with Columbia near the end of 1985. Def Jam's agreement with Columbia was known as a label deal. Simmons and Rubin would have almost complete control over their label. Def Jam would have its own offices and employees. It would be responsible for finding artists, subject to Columbia's approval. In return, CBS (the media network that owned Columbia at the time) owned the master copies of the recordings and would pay Def Jam royalties (money based on sales of the recordings). Simmons and Rubin would not make a huge amount of money out of the agreement. But at the time, "it was the greatest opportunity in the whole world," Simmons recalled.

Def Jam closed its $2 million multi-album deal with CBS in September. To celebrate, Simmons and Rubin threw a "White Castle" party on the roof of the hip club Danceteria. A Def Jam staffer delivered two thousand hamburgers from the White Castle fast-food chain to the party by cab. Most of the burgers were stuffed inside the car, with the rest tied to the roof.

Despite the agreement, the conservative CBS executives were skeptical. At the celebration party, they discussed among themselves whether hip-hop really counted as music. Then the Beastie Boys arrived and started a food fight, during which CBS's chairman, Walter

The term *def* came from Rick Rubin's misunderstanding of the slang he heard in New York's hip-hop clubs. Young African Americans used the term *death* to mean "the best." But Rubin thought the word he heard was *def*.

Yetnikoff, got hit in the head with a cheeseburger. Remarkably, the deal still went through.

Elizabeth Street

In June 1985, Simmons and Rubin spent a chunk of their $600,000 advance (money that pays for the making of an album) from Columbia to buy a building on Elizabeth Street in the East Village neighborhood of Manhattan. The former machine shop was in a rough area of the East Village. Crack—a new form of smokable cocaine that had overtaken New York—was sold everywhere. One staffer recalled that the streets practically sparkled with glass fragments from car windows smashed by drug addicts looking for radios to steal for money.

The building needed some serious repairs. But eventually, Rush Management moved into the first floor of the building. Def Jam settled into the second, and Rubin took an apartment on the third. (Rubin had hoped to share the third-floor apartment with Simmons, to improve their communication. But renovations took so long that Simmons ended up buying a penthouse apartment in another building.) The new headquarters of both of Simmons's businesses was "small, cramped, and incredibly creative," Simmons recalled.

In December 1985, Def Jam released its first full-length album: LL Cool J's *Radio*. The album had hardly any melodies, just hard beats and rhyming—and both critics and consumers loved it. On the strength of songs such as "I Can't Live Without My Radio" and "Rock the Bells," *Radio* went gold. It was an astonishing accomplishment for a new artist in a new genre and a very promising start for the new label.

Rock and Rap

As Def Jam took off, Simmons kept an eye on the artists being managed by Rush—particularly Run-D.M.C. Simmons asked Rubin to coproduce Run-D.M.C.'s third album, *Raising Hell.* For one of the songs, Simmons and Run wanted to sample a rock record they remembered from the 1970s. But they could not remember the name of the band or the song. Rubin understood immediately what record they meant. It was "Walk This Way" by Aerosmith. But rather than just sampling the song, Rubin contacted Aerosmith and arranged for the band to come into the studio. Together, Run-D.M.C. and Aerosmith recorded a rap version of the rock classic.

Rap rock: Run *(left)* of Run-D.M.C poses with Steven Tyler of Aerosmith at the MTV Video Music Awards in 1999. Aerosmith and Run-D.M.C. recorded a rap version of the song "Walk This Way."

The song was a hit. The new "Walk This Way" went to number four on the *Billboard* chart, making it the first rap song to break the top five. *Raising Hell* sold 2.5 million copies.

"Walk This Way" had a huge impact on the careers of everyone who worked on it. It made Run-D.M.C. into a group that could pack arenas. It revived Aerosmith's musical career, which had been in a slump. It made Rubin a world-class producer and Simmons a world-class manager. The song also finally got Run-D.M.C. onto MTV, the music video channel. Founded in 1981, MTV had resisted playing hip-hop videos for five years. For the first time, hip-hop was seen as a crossover genre.

Krush Groove

Simmons had the idea to make a movie about his most successful act, Run-D.M.C. By then a few hip-hop movies had already been made, such as *Breakin'* (1984) and *Beat Street* (1984). Simmons pitched his idea to several Hollywood producers with no success. Eventually, he made a deal with a young African American producer, George Jackson, and a young African American director, Michael Schultz. Schultz suggested the film's plot should not center on Run-D.M.C. but rather on the founding of Def Jam.

Simmons agreed—as long as the artists with Def Jam and Rush Management would be a major part of the film. "Russell really cared about finding new ways to expose the music to a bigger audience," Rubin recalled. Once the script for *Krush Groove* was complete, the hero of the story had become Russell Walker, a character based on Simmons.

Simmons and his partners managed to get a deal with Warner Brothers to make the film. In the thinly plotted film, Russell Walker is forced to borrow money from a shady character to make Run-D.M.C.'s records. At the same time, Walker and his brother Run both try to win

On the big screen: Run-D.M.C. as they appeared in the 1985 film *Krush Groove* (1985). The movie depicted the founding of Def Jam.

the heart of R & B singer Sheila E. Almost everyone appeared as themselves in the film, even Rubin. The only exception was Simmons, who was played by a professional actor, Blair Underwood, in his feature-film debut. Simmons had a small role as a club owner named Crocket.

In one famous scene, the characters Russell and Rick meet with a loan officer in a bank to try to get the money they need to press records. When the loan officer says that he is unfamiliar with rap music, Russell and Rick demonstrate it at the top of their lungs. The bank's customers stare in shock. "*Krush Groove* was really almost our story," Simmons said later. "That movie is as stupid as we were."

The film received lukewarm reviews but grossed $11 million. Simmons, however, received just $15,000 and an associate producer's credit for his work. "I have to chalk that one up to experience," he recalled thinking.

Dissatisfied with the quality of *Krush Groove*, Simmons and Rubin decided to make another hip-hop film that would be closer to their vision. The two formed their own production company, Def Pictures, and started work on *Tougher Than Leather*. Their next film would center on Run-D.M.C.

Golden Age

While Simmons's Hollywood debut was less than spectacular, things could not have been going better for Def Jam. For Simmons the period from about 1986 to 1990 was "Def Jam's first golden era." By then the label had added political rappers Public Enemy and rap-battle-veteran

Public Enemy's first album, *Yo! Bum Rush the Show*, came out in 1987. It was Def Jam's most politically charged release to that point. Head rapper Chuck D (Carleton Douglas Ridenhour) and his crew tackled race relations and police violence.

Bum rush the label: Political rap group Public Enemy *(above)* joined Def Jam in 1986.

Slick Rick to its roster. "Each was different, yet they all shared a vision of pushing the creative envelope while remaining honest to themselves," Simmons recalled.

Meanwhile, Rush Management was doing equally well with artists who recorded for other labels, especially Run-D.M.C. In the summer of 1986, Run-D.M.C.'s *Raising Hell* went platinum, selling a million copies—a first for a hip-hop record.

The following year, 1987, was a banner year for Def Jam. LL Cool J's second album, *Bigger and Deffer*, went triple platinum. The Beastie Boys' first album, *Licensed to Ill*, did even better, selling four million records. For a new genre like hip-hop, these sales figures were almost unbelievable. Columbia's gamble on the unknown world of hip-hop had paid off massively: two of its three top-selling releases in 1987 came from Def Jam.

Altogether, Def Jam had sold more than eight million records in its short history. Music executives were finally beginning to believe that hip-hop was not just a passing fad. In 1987 Simmons told the *New York Times*, "Rap will be a fixture the way jazz and rock and roll are."

USA TODAY.
A GANNETT COMPANY

CHAPTER FOUR

Hashing it out: Simmons at his desk in 1990, the year he said was the coldest in Def Jam history. The late 1980s brought organizational problems and new competition to the label.

The Cold Years

■■■■■

Despite Def Jam's success—or perhaps because of it—the company was experiencing growing pains by the late 1980s. Def Jam had been informal from its founding in an NYU dorm room. This remained the case even as the label grew. There were few written contracts with producers, writers, or musicians hired for recording sessions. At more established labels, agreements would be put in writing and checked by lawyers.

Def Jam was also run in a disorganized way. In 1988 one top employee wrote to Simmons and Rubin that Def Jam was "in a state of total disarray, complete with a [bad] attitude toward management, administration, signing, spending, hiring, artists, and teamwork." The employee accused Simmons and Rubin of being more interested in producing records than in running the company well.

Adding to the disorganization, Simmons often made little distinction between Def Jam and Rush Management. Money moved back and forth between the two. The attitude was to do whatever was necessary to promote the music. But not keeping good accounting records can cost a company money—and can even be illegal.

These are common problems for small businesses that achieve success too quickly. But Simmons and Rubin were beginning to grow apart musically as well. Simmons was getting back in touch with the gritty R & B that he had enjoyed before he discovered hip-hop. He signed acts such as Oran "Juice" Jones, Chuck Stanley, and Alyson Williams.

Meanwhile, Rubin was returning to his first love: rock. This led him to decide to sign Slayer, a band whose music was about as different from hip-hop as possible. Slayer's music was an extremely aggressive kind of rock known as thrash metal or speed metal. The band's previous two albums, *Show No Mercy* and *Hell Awaits*, were full of songs about hell and the devil.

For a record label as small as Def Jam, having such a wide-ranging, inconsistent lineup of artists made little sense. While Simmons was focusing on his R & B artists and Rubin on rock, both neglected hip-hop acts that they had signed together, such as Public Enemy. Simmons and Rubin rarely attended the same meetings. Each made decisions without consulting the other. Both preferred working from home rather than going into the office. Simmons usually held meetings with Def Jam staff by speakerphone.

Def Jam also faced new competition from other small hip-hop labels—such as First Priority and Jive—that had signed distribution agreements with major labels. The "Def Jam sound" was no longer enough. Radio stations still played rap only at certain limited times. With the added competition, Simmons and his promotion staff had to fight even harder to get Def Jam's records heard.

Simmons was unhappy about his splintering relationship with Rubin. Adding to his worries, Run-D.M.C.'s career seemed to be slowing down. The group was suing Profile Records to release them from their recording contract so they could sign with Def Jam. The lawsuit held up their fourth album, *Tougher Than Leather*. When the suit was finally settled in 1988, Run-D.M.C. was not able to make the break to Def Jam and remained with Profile.

Meanwhile, Simmons had not cut back on his heavy drug use. His drug of choice was cocaine rolled in cigarettes. But he had not entirely given up his old drug of choice, PCP, either. At one meeting held at Simmons's apartment, a Def Jam employee went to his freezer looking for ice and found instead a pile of red packages. When Simmons was asked what they were, he replied matter-of-factly, "Dust."

Tougher Than Leather

In September 1988, after nearly two years of work, the film *Tougher Than Leather* was finally released. Simmons, Rubin, and the three members of Run-D.M.C. had split the cost of making it. Various film distributors had been interested in the project in theory. But once they saw the completed film, they changed their minds. Simmons had planned for the film to coincide with the release of Run-D.M.C.'s album and a biography of the group—all called *Tougher Than Leather*—but the release dates did not come together.

The film's main plot centered on Run-D.M.C. being hassled by gangsters. The Beastie Boys and Slick Rick appeared, as did Simmons. He played himself this time, and Rubin played bad guy Vic Ferrante. Rubin was also the film's director. In some ways, the film seemed frozen in time. The Beastie Boys played an up-and-coming group in the film, but by the time of its release, they were megastars and had left Def Jam for a major label.

Biopic: Director Rick Rubin *(foreground)* and cinematographer Feliks Parnell *(far right)* with Run-D.M.C. on the set of the movie *Tougher Than Leather* (1988).

The advance press for the movie was huge, which made the bad reviews that came later all the more painful. Rubin used a racial slur several times in the film, which many critics found difficult to stomach. The film was also criticized for its unnecessary nudity and violence. Richard Harrington of the *Washington Post* newspaper described *Tougher Than Leather* as "vile, vicious, despicable, stupid, sexist, racist, and horrendously made."

Simmons was dismayed by his failed attempts at filmmaking, especially in contrast to his successes in the music business. "Both experiences were so much fun that I never wanted to make a movie again," he recalled in his autobiography.

Alone at Def Jam

About the same time that *Tougher Than Leather* was released, the conflict between Simmons and Rubin came to a head. "We'd been stepping on each other's toes a lot, kind of growing apart creatively, no communication," Rubin recalled. "I felt like my vision was being compromised, and I was sure he felt like his was."

Rubin suggested they meet for lunch to talk about the company's future. Rubin asked Simmons if he wanted to leave. When Simmons said no, Rubin said he would go instead. The partners agreed that Rubin would retain a large financial stake in Def Jam but no creative or managerial input. Like many agreements at Def Jam, the split was purely verbal.

"The parting was difficult for Def Jam, since many of the acts and personnel had been signed by Rick," Simmons recalled. Some of the acts that really did not fit Simmons's vision—Slayer, the Black Crowes, and controversial comedian Andrew Dice Clay—were released from their contracts and joined Rubin's new label, Def American.

Columbia, Def Jam's major-label distributor, took the news in stride. "Russell's been a winner since day one," Ruben Rodriguez, an executive at Columbia, recalled. "Plus, the face of Def Jam was Russell. You never want to see a combination like that break up, but . . . I felt Russell could stand on his own." Simmons was equally confident he could run the company by himself.

 In 1993 Rick Rubin changed the name of Def American to American Recordings. Rubin sought the change after learning that *def* had entered a dictionary. He believed the term had lost its edge.

Rush Communications

After Rubin's departure, Simmons realized that his organizations could no longer function as loosely as they had in the past. He needed to draw a firm distinction between Def Jam and Rush Management. His solution was to create a parent company, Rush Communications, which included Def Jam and Rush Management under its umbrella. The goal was to help both organizations run more smoothly and legally.

At the same time, Simmons was trying to renegotiate Def Jam's relationship with Sony, which bought Columbia in 1989. "We'd made Def Jam the most important real brand in hip-hop," Simmons recalled. "Our roster of LL Cool J, the Beastie Boys, Slick Rick, and Public Enemy was the best in the game."

Def Jam had sold millions of records. But Simmons had not benefited financially as much as he would have liked. He was able to negotiate a new deal, in which Sony bought a 50 percent share in Def Jam. In exchange, Def Jam received bigger advances, higher royalty rates, and more money for staff.

Meanwhile, Simmons continued to make time for what he did best: promotion. One employee remembered a ritual Simmons did nearly every day. He would sit down on the couch with a bag of potato chips and call radio programmers, pressing them to play Def Jam records, for three hours straight. He had long since given up needing a phone book. He could dial all their numbers from memory.

Former partners: Lyor Cohen *(left)* and Russell Simmons attend the 2011 White House Correspondents' Association Dinner. Cohen began working for Rush Management in 1985.

Rush Associated Labels

"The coldest year in Def Jam's history was probably 1990," Simmons wrote in his autobiography. Early that year, he and Lyor Cohen launched a new venture, Rush Associated Labels (RAL). Cohen had previously worked as Run-D.M.C.'s road

IN FOCUS

Lyor Cohen

Lyor Cohen entered the music industry as a club promoter in Los Angeles. His first encounter with Def Jam artists came in 1984, when Cohen booked a Run-D.M.C. concert. In 1985 Cohen moved to New York City in search of a new job. He quickly became Run-D.M.C.'s road manager. By the year's end, Cohen had joined the Rush Management staff full-time.

Cohen was a fan of *The Art of War*, an ancient Chinese guide to military strategies. He applied many of its lessons to artist management. Cohen often behaved like a general in the office, angrily shouting orders. His "take-no-prisoners" approach to business sometimes alienated people in the industry—including some Def Jam employees—but it also helped Def Jam artists make more money. He sought out endorsement deals and would stay behind after concerts to make sure artists received fair deals from show promoters. His tough tactics complemented Simmons's relentless hyping of Def Jam releases.

By the start of 1988, Cohen had become Rush Management's chief operating officer. He would later become Def Jam's president. In the 1990s, Cohen negotiated a deal with Jay-Z's Roc-A-Fella Records that brought one of hip-hop's future legends to Def Jam. As of 2011, Cohen was head of Warner Music Group.

manager and had taken a leadership role in Rush Management by the late 1980s.

RAL included several smaller record labels that shared Def Jam as their mother label—similar to the way Columbia and other major labels had smaller labels under their umbrella. But not a single one of the RAL labels succeeded. Simmons had imagined these labels as a new source of revenue—but rather than bringing in money, the labels got Def Jam deeply in debt to Sony. Later, Simmons described Rush Associated Labels as simply "a mistake."

Hip-hop music was continuing to evolve at lightning speed. Def

Jam had set the standard for East Coast hip-hop. But the West Coast was catching up. In 1989 a rap group called N.W.A. from Los Angeles, California, released *Straight Outta Compton*. Named after Compton, a rough Los Angeles neighborhood, the groundbreaking album put gangsta rap on the map.

The lyrics of West Coast rap groups were much more violent than what was coming out of the East Coast. At the same time, the music was more melodic. And despite that most gangsta rap songs were too offensive to be played on the radio, the albums sold in the millions. As Simmons recalled, "We in New York were no longer making what America wanted to hear, and [Los Angeles] was."

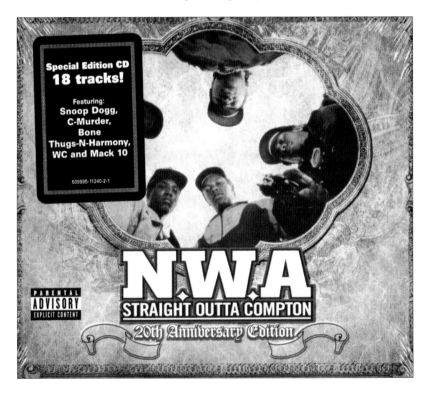

Pioneering record: *Straight Outta Compton* by N.W.A. was a historic album in gangsta rap. The 20th Anniversary Edition CD box set was released in December 2007.

January 2, 1991

'Gangsta' rap reflects an urban jungle

<u>From the Pages of</u>
<u>USA TODAY</u>

M.C. Hammer and Vanilla Ice may have ended the year topping the pop charts, but "gangsta" rappers—grim storytellers of inner-city violence and sex—rule the rap world. Born in Los Angeles' gang-torn streets, gangsta rap portrays itself as the 6 o'clock news put to vinyl. The music crackles with gunfire. As gangsta pioneers N.W.A. say in "Gangsta, Gangsta": "I got a shotgun, and here's the plot/takin' (expletive) out with a flurry of buckshots."

Last year saw gangsta rap's popularity soar. Ice Cube (*AmeriKKKa's Most Wanted*), Luke featuring the 2 Live Crew (*Banned in the U.S.A.*) and N.W.A. (*100 Miles and Runnin'*) made top 30 on pop charts.

Are they street heroes or negative role models? For a frustrated generation of inner-city youth, they're both. "It's negative in a way, but it lets you know what's going on in reality," says Kevin Lee, 19, of Lake Arbor, Md. "In that sense, it's positive." Says Terrance Thorne, 21, of Capital Heights, Md.: "When someone gets on our nerves, I listen to it and think there's enough killing."

Not all gangsta rap is negative. Several acts joined to record "We're All in the Same Gang," an anti-gang song that made *Billboard's* R & B top 40 this summer. But the rap offshoot has parents worried. Jamie Brown publishes *Sister to Sister*, a Washington, D.C.-based magazine that covers rap and R & B. She became concerned when one of her two teen sons playfully pointed a finger at her head and recited lyrics from Kool G Rap and D.J. Polo's Streets of New York: "I also have a .38."

"I don't even think it's music," Brown says. "It preaches disunity between black males and females, and harming one another physically." Brown has been printing gangsta rap lyrics in her magazine to show parents what their children are hearing. "What bothers me is that it's really their reality," Brown says. "When I saw N.W.A., I thought 'Our children are going through this?' It's good people are made aware of it, but not the kids."

But that's what the kids want to hear, Ice T says. "My stuff is not for the squeamish or very prudish. It is for street people who hang out. "They want to hear me," he says, not M.C. Hammer.

—James T. Jones IV

Hollywood Shuffle

Despite his early difficulties in film, Simmons was determined to keep trying to break into the industry. Through his connections in Hollywood, he was able to read the script of John Singleton's *Boyz n the Hood*. *Boyz* was the story of three young African American men struggling to survive their violent inner-city environment.

At the time, Columbia Studios already owned the script. But the executives were not moving forward with making a film out of it. To Simmons the script's potential was absolutely obvious. He hoped to produce the movie.

Boyz: Morris Chestnut *(left)*, Cuba Gooding Jr. *(center)*, and Ice Cube *(right)* in *Boyz n the Hood* (1991). Simmons hoped to produce the movie but was dropped from the project.

With Simmons interested, Columbia was also suddenly interested. But in the negotiations, Sony dropped Simmons from the project. *Boyz*, released in 1991, starred Cuba Gooding Jr., Ice Cube, and Laurence Fishburne. It went on to be nominated for two Academy Awards: best director and best original screenplay.

According to an article in *Black Enterprise* magazine, Simmons's refusal to compromise his hip-hop style caught up with him during *Boyz* negotiations. The president of Columbia Studios was hesitant to set up a film deal with "a man who came to meetings dressed like [an office] messenger and whose conversation was filled with the rawest

IN F⊕CUS

Professor Griff

In 1989 Public Enemy was suddenly in the headlines for an ugly reason. One of its members, Professor Griff, had made an anti-Semitic remark in an interview with the *Washington Post*. The Jewish community was outraged. Public Enemy made the situation worse by releasing "Welcome to the Terrordome." A lyric in the song compared the Jewish community's criticism of Public Enemy to the crucifixion of Jesus. Various boycotts of Public Enemy followed.

Soon afterward, Professor Griff had a confrontation with the white rap group 3rd Bass in the Def Jam office. Griff used an anti-Semitic slur and a fight broke out, during which the office was severely damaged.

Simmons released a public statement after the incident. "I don't like Professor Griff and I hate what he stands for. He's not allowed anymore in the offices of Def Jam. Griff's

wildest imaginary Jewish conspiracy could not have done more damage to Public Enemy than has Griff himself." Despite the controversy, in 1992 Public Enemy was still Def Jam's number one act.

Controversy: Professor Griff of Public Enemy, a Def Jam group, performs in 1990. Griff made a number of anti-Semitic remarks.

of obscenities." Simmons was unapologetic. "It's very important to me that my persona, my clothes, my whole outlook is one that shows black kids on the way up that the Cosby way or look [that is, the behavior and appearance of wholesome African American comedian Bill Cosby] is not the only successful black image that's available for them

Television: DJ Jazzy Jeff *(left)* and the Fresh Prince (Will Smith) are pictured in the 1980s. Simmons tried to get Smith a television deal, but Smith ended up landing the deal on his own.

to emulate," he told *Black Enterprise.*

Simmons also tried to develop film and television projects for Will Smith. Smith was then an aspiring actor. Most people knew him better as the Fresh Prince of DJ Jazzy Jeff and the Fresh Prince, a hip-hop group represented by Rush. Smith eventually landed a deal for a television series, *The Fresh Prince of Bel-Air*, without Simmons's involvement. (Aware that Simmons had worked hard to try to find him acting projects, Smith sent him a check for $250,000 to get out of his management deal.)

Simmons later admitted that it was tough to succeed in Hollywood when he was based in New York. Trying to run Def Jam and Rush at the same time only made it harder. While most Hollywood people were dedicated full-time to making deals, Simmons said, he was "only half-way paying attention."

Comedy: Russell Simmons, seen here in 1995, noticed a growing comedy scene in the early 1990s. He came up with the idea of having a television show with African American stand-up comedians.

A New Direction

In the early 1990s, Simmons discovered another exciting scene that the rest of the country didn't know about. At venues such as the Comedy Act Theater in Los Angeles and the Uptown Comedy Club in Harlem, Simmons saw a group of cutting-edge African American comedians performing in front of a young, hip-hop audience. Simmons also noticed that many music clubs became comedy clubs one night of the week—and that those nights were almost always sold out.

Stand-up comedy had been around for decades. Many well-known African American comedians—Bill Cosby, Richard Pryor, and Eddie Murphy—had gotten their start doing stand-up. But Simmons hadn't discovered one talented performer—he had discovered a whole scene. The comedians were unknown, uncensored, and undeniably funny. Simmons knew that these comedians would have wide appeal if only they could reach a mass audience. "A light bulb went on," Simmons recalled. "The commonsense thing to do was to expose this to everyone." He came up with the idea of a television show featuring young African American stand-up comedians.

To pitch his idea, Simmons found three partners: Stan Lathan, an established director and producer, and Bernie Brillstein and Brad Grey of the management and production company Brillstein-Grey. Lathan had directed the early hip-hop film *Beat Street* in addition to many television programs. Brillstein and Grey had produced successful comedies such as *Ghostbusters* and *Wayne's World*.

Entertainer: Martin Lawrence at the MTV Video Music Awards in 1993. Lawrence hosted Simmons's stand-up comedy television show.

Simmons and his partners formed a new company, SLBG. SLBG planned to produce the comedy show and comanage the comedians they discovered. Lathan and Simmons would scout the comedians, while Brillstein and Grey would use their connections in the television industry to get the show on the air.

The premise of the thirty-minute show was simple: four stand-up comedians would be taped performing in front of a live audience. The show would be hosted by another up-and-coming African American comedian, Martin Lawrence. When SLBG pitched the idea to cable channel HBO, they won a contract to do four shows with sixteen comedians.

Simmons's involvement was crucial to HBO's decision. "We knew what Russell had done in the music world, and the effect of the hip-hop world on style, fashion, culture, and language," Bridget Potter, senior vice president of original programming at HBO, recalled. "If comedy was going to be part of that world, then we knew it was something that could work for HBO."

Def Comedy Jam first aired on HBO in August 1992. The show premiered on HBO's Friday midnight time slot. The language was raw, and the subject matter was adults-only. "Virtually every joke is unprintable," wrote one reviewer for the *New York Times*. A DJ accompanied the comedy routines, scratching records in the background. The show was an instant hit with HBO viewers. It also beat the late-night classic *The Tonight Show* in the ratings.

Despite *Def Comedy Jam*'s success, Simmons found himself fielding criticism from people who were offended by the adult content and what they saw as negative portrayals of black people. Bill Cosby and Afro-Caribbean actor Sidney Poitier said publicly that they were offended by the show's language. "When you're a Cosby or Poitier you

Hip-hop stand-up: Comedian D. L. Hughley performs on *Russell Simmons' Def Comedy Jam* in 2007. It aired on HBO.

March 6, 1992

Raunchy, rowdy *Def Comedy*

<u>From the Pages of</u>
<u>USA TODAY</u>

To be young, gifted, black ... and nasty, very nasty. This will get you a spot on HBO's newest late-night showcase for stand-up humor so cutting-edge raw you could split open a vein.

It's a rare comic on *Russell Simmons' Def Comedy Jam* who doesn't [hurl] profanities at gale force to a rowdy audience that never actually rolls in the aisle. That's because they're too busy leaping from their seats in an ecstasy of "giving it up." Blessed by a charismatic host (Martin Lawrence), this eight-week anthology offers a window on a hip-hop world, a vivid pop-culture gospel rendered in 12-letter unprintables.

Don't be surprised if Simmons, a rap mogul whose Def Jam label gave us the likes of Public Enemy and Run-D.M.C., has another hit on his hands. By not letting any of these on-the-rise comedians overstay their welcome, he's sure to leave anyone with a taste for this wild stuff wanting more. But because four acts are crammed into each half-hour, almost no one is able to hit a performance stride, giving the show a profane sameness. Most distinctive of the two episodes made available is Reggie McFadden's hysterical physical comedy in week two.

Throughout, Lawrence and several of the other comics make pointed reference to the fact that by being on a mainstream outlet like pay-cable giant HBO, chances are white people will be watching in shock and bafflement. HBO warns that this material is for adults only, which is pretty silly. *Def Comedy Jam* is for long-stunted adolescents only. A real adult would want nothing to do with it.

—Matt Roush

think it's a good idea to make everybody believe we're all doctors and lawyers," Simmons recalled. "*Def Comedy* was so raw, so honest, so uncensored, it made people who worried about 'positive' black images very uncomfortable. Which meant the show did its job."

Def Comedy Jam spawned a live tour beginning in 1993. Many *Def Comedy* performers went on to greater fame, including Dave

Chappelle, Chris Rock, Cedric the Entertainer, Steve Harvey, Bernie Mac, and Jamie Foxx.

Phat Farm

After his relationship with Paulette Mims had ended, Simmons had developed a reputation as a ladies' man. He became fond of dating fashion models—sometimes more than one at a time.

Over the years, Simmons had unintentionally picked up a lot of insider information about the modeling business. In the early 1990s, he even briefly considered opening his own modeling agency. Simmons also learned a lot about the business of fashion from his model girl-

Dress like Simmons: A model wears clothes from Phat Farm at the 2002 MTV Fashionably Loud show. Phat Farm is a hip-hop clothing line Simmons created in 1992.

friends. After meeting with clothing buyers and designers, Simmons decided to launch his own hip-hop clothing line.

By the early 1990s, hip-hop fashion was in transition, and so was Simmons's own look. As a young record promoter and record label founder, he had been known for his hip-hop uniform of sweatsuits and unlaced Adidas shoes. But preppy clothing was starting to make its way into street fashion. Simmons's wardrobe grew to include clothes that were neat, traditional, and expensive looking.

Simmons wanted his fashion line to appeal to people like himself—someone who had grown up with hip-hop

Dress Code

In 1992 Simmons was featured on the cover of *Black Enterprise* wearing his hip-hop uniform—a university hoodie, jeans, and high-top sneakers—while sitting on the hood of a Rolls-Royce. The headline blared, "How This 35-Year-Old CEO Built a $34 Million Rap Empire." It was a first for the conservative business magazine.

Two years later, rapper and entrepreneur Sean Combs (then known as Puff Daddy and later P. Diddy or Diddy) held a twenty-fourth birthday party at the Roseland Ballroom in Manhattan. The invitation spelled out the party's dress code, banning sneakers, jeans, and T-shirts. "This code applies to everyone," it stated. "P.S. There will be one exception, Russell Simmons."

but no longer wanted to dress like a teenager. "It was supposed to be more upscale," he recalled, "the kind of clothes I liked and wore."

Simmons envisioned a clothing line in a preppy style, made of high-quality fabric, but with a hip-hop influence—a looser cut and, most important, conspicuous logos. "Hip-hop culture was born in poor neighborhoods where people dream of owning things that instantly confer status—the right clothes, hot logos, brand names," he explained. For a black-owned clothing company, it was a unique approach. Bringing together urban slang—*phat* meaning "cool"—with country-club style, he decided to name his line Phat Farm.

His partner in this venture was Mark Beguda, the owner of an expensive boutique where Simmons often bought his girlfriends' dresses. Simmons brought his knowledge of street fashion, while Beguda brought his experience in fashion retailing. Together, they opened the first Phat Farm store in New York City's SoHo neighborhood in 1993.

At the time, Simmons planned to start small, with one boutique, and see how far he could go. "It's fun and I can afford to do it," he said shortly after the store opened. "So if I lose a lot of money on it, I had fun. If I make money, I'll have even more fun."

The first Phat Farm line, which included about fifty items, was designed by Alyasha Jibril Owerka-Moore and Eli Morgan Gesner. Both were twenty-two years old, former graffiti artists, and untrained in fashion. The prices ranged from $25 for a T-shirt to $650 for a leather jacket. The store did a brisk business on its first day. Among the customers was female hip-hop pioneer Queen Latifah.

White Elephant

Simmons initially invested $500,000 in Phat Farm. Despite the media coverage and the initial sales rush, the company wasn't an immediate hit. Still, Simmons continued to invest in it. He was convinced that he was right about hip-hop fashion, just as he had been right about hip-hop music and hip-hop comedy.

Part of Phat Farm's marketing strategy was not to sell to the ethnic sections in department stores or to smaller stores that catered exclusively to African American customers. Simmons wanted the clothing line to appeal to a broad market. "A lot of these clothes could be worn by a sixty-year-old Jewish guy," he told the *New York Times*.

In the early years, this policy meant that Phat Farm clothing was not widely available. To Simmons, that was a selling point. "Our philosophy has always been that we wouldn't sell to just anybody, and we purposely stayed limited in our distribution," he said. He recalled his citywide searches for the right sneakers as a young man—no matter what the cost—and how the search only increased his enjoyment.

In *Life and Def*, Simmons imagined a hypothetical customer having to travel for hours to get to the one boutique that carried Phat Farm— only to discover he could not afford a $100 rugby shirt and having to settle for a $50 T-shirt. "It's too bad that you couldn't get the rugby shirt that day, but you have to respect a brand that does that to you," he wrote.

New Passions

In the 1990s, Simmons developed two new passions. The first was technology. He was an early fan of using faxes and cell phones to work from home, his car, or other places, rather than going into his Def Jam office, which he rarely did. "Way before it was commonplace, my cell phone was my desk," he recalled. On the cover of his autobiography *Life and Def*, Simmons is pictured in a typical pose. He's in the backseat of a car, a cell phone with earphones in one hand and a BlackBerry (a wireless communications device) in the other.

He also got hooked on the stairclimber (an exercise machine), spending hours on it every day. He would even hold meetings while working out, huffing and puffing as he talked to people by speakerphone.

During the mid-1990s, Simmons sank $10 million into Phat Farm. Whenever he invested more money, he had a moment of intense doubt. His lowest moment came in 1994, when he signed a licensing deal with USA Classics. According to the deal, USA Classics bought the rights to the Phat Farm name and logo. It would design and manufacture the clothing, under Phat Farm's supervision and pay Phat Farm a percentage.

Then USA Classics went bankrupt. Simmons had to buy back the licensing rights, which USA Classics owned despite its bankruptcy. "I know my friends thought I was stupid and that Phat Farm was a white elephant [a business that costs so much to maintain, it will never be profitable]," he recalled in his autobiography. "Yet all that time I was learning. . . . I put the time in and paid attention."

Kimora Lee

In 1994 Simmons was attending a fashion show that was part of New

York's annual Fashion Week. Backstage he met Kimora Lee, a seventeen-year-old model from Saint Louis, Missouri. Simmons was nearly twenty years older than she. Despite the age difference, he was impressed by how worldly Lee was.

The daughter of an African American father and an Asian mother, Lee was more than 6 feet (1.8 meters) tall and stunning. She had been a professional model since the age of thirteen. "She had lived all over the world," Simmons recalled later. "She spoke a bunch of languages—French, German, Italian, Japanese. She had a certain polish and sophistication, and she was and is a lot of fun."

A couple: Kimora Lee *(left)* and Russell attend a movie premiere together in New York in 1999. The two met in 1994, when Lee was seventeen.

The other models warned Lee to stay away from Simmons, saying he was too old for her. But Lee's mother gave her approval to the relationship. "I was very mature for my age, and Russell has always been very playful and young at heart," Lee recalled.

Sale of Def Jam

By the mid-1990s, Simmons had mostly removed himself from the daily running of Def Jam. But he had left the label in the care of Lyor Cohen and other talented employees. "The truth is, the more I got

IN FOCUS

Giving Back

In the early 1990s, Joseph Simmons, aka Run of Run-D.M.C., became a Christian minister and grew interested in giving back to the community. His brothers, Russell and Danny, shared a similar interest in philanthropy, or charitable work. In 1995 the three brothers founded the Rush Philanthropic Arts Foundation. The foundation works to introduce the arts to underprivileged kids. It also helps artists of color gain exposure for their work.

away from Def Jam on a day-to-day basis, the better the company did," Simmons recalled.

One role Simmons did not hand over to Cohen was managing Def Jam's relationship with its major-label distributor, Sony. For years, this relationship had been difficult. Simmons and the executives at Sony constantly argued about the fees that Sony deducted from Def Jam's share of the profits. And Simmons felt deeply betrayed when Sony approached some of Def Jam's earliest artists, such as LL Cool J and Public Enemy, to try to convince them to sign directly with Sony. By 1994 Sony wanted to buy Simmons out or otherwise convince him to leave Def Jam.

For many small record labels, such a difficult period might have spelled the end. But Simmons had made a smart decision in naming his comedy show *Def Comedy Jam*. The show was a runaway success, and that made the name *Def Jam* stand for more than just a struggling independent record label. Because of the hit show, *Def Jam* remained a high-profile, high-profit brand in the urban community. "Connecting *Def Comedy Jam* to Def Jam records helped both entities—associating HBO with an established hip-hop brand helped get the show on the air, while linking the label to a hot TV show helped the label survive a cold period," Simmons recalled.

Meanwhile, the major label PolyGram (which years ago had given Kurtis Blow his first big break) wanted to become a force in hip-hop. As Simmons recalled later, PolyGram executives knew very little about the genre. They were familiar with Def Jam's name and its artists, and they knew its contract with Sony was ending. But they had no idea that Def Jam was $17 million in debt to Sony.

In his negotiations with PolyGram, Lyor Cohen and Simmons were somewhat creative with the truth. "The trick of the deal for us was to not let PolyGram know how badly we needed the money," he recalled. Cohen and Simmons led PolyGram to believe that Sony and other record companies were in a bidding war for Def Jam.

Eventually, PolyGram paid $35 million for a 50 percent stake in Def Jam. As part of the deal, Rush Management was dissolved. Rush Associated Labels was folded into Def Jam. After paying Sony and various lawyers' and accountants' fees, Simmons, Rick Rubin, and Lyor Cohen walked away with $15 million.

"In 1994, Russell was the kind of hip-hop executive that all of his peers in the industry aspired to be," Stacy Gueraseva wrote in *Def Jam, Inc.*, a book about the label's history. "He had the three desirable components: money, power, and respect." He had been through some difficult years, but once again, Simmons was back on top.

The agreement not only meant Def Jam would live to see another decade. It also marked a new phase in Simmons's life. Up to this point, his business interests had already been fairly wide-ranging. They encompassed film, television, comedy, and fashion, as well as music. But now he was set to diversify his businesses more than anyone could have thought possible.

On top: Simmons on a New York City rooftop in 2003. He pursued new business directions in the twenty-first century.

A Hip-Hop Life

"In the '80s I spent most of my time promoting hip-hop music," Simmons wrote in *Life and Def.* "In the '90s I used that success to expand the reach of hip-hop culture." The 1990s was a period of constant change for Simmons. If he wasn't launching a new business, he was closing down or selling off an old one.

Even as he was tracking his wide-ranging business ventures, Simmons made time to become more politically active. His businesses helped sponsor marches, voter registration drives, and other political activities. To an outside observer, his diverse projects would seem to have little in common. But to Simmons, the link was clear. All of his businesses and all of his political campaigns were tied together by their connection to a young, urban, hip-hop lifestyle.

Film Producer

By the mid-1990s, Simmons had moved to Los Angeles. He began to achieve some success as a film producer. Among his new projects was *The Addiction* (1995), a vampire film with an artistic sensibility. The film's director, Abel Ferrara, shot it in black and white. Unlike in most vampire movies, in *The Addiction*, blood is a metaphor for heroin. The film enjoyed limited success. "While I'm not sure that anyone else would agree with me, I'm very proud of that film as an artistic accomplishment," Simmons recalled.

Hollywood artist: Director Abel Ferrara in Florida in 2009. Simmons produced Ferrara's film *The Addiction* (1995).

His next film was the polar opposite—an African American version of the 1963 comedy classic *The Nutty Professor*. Simmons worked with an established Hollywood producer, Brian Grazer, on the project. The starring role went to Eddie Murphy.

As coproducer, Simmons commented on drafts of the

MENDELIAN INHERITANCE   HYBRIDIZATION

AUTOSOMAL RECESSIVE
AUTOSOMAL DOMINANT
X-LINKED
POLYGENIC

$dd\,H_2O = 5.0\,mL$
$20\%\,PEG = 0.5\,mL$
$20x\,SSPE = 1.0\,mL$
$20\%\,SDS = 3.5\,n$

$10\,ml$

Bad chemistry: Eddie Murphy in *The Nutty Professor* (1996). After conflicts with other producers on this film, Simmons was not invited to its premiere.

script. But he had little direct involvement once the script was complete. His trademark hands-off approach had been successful in most of his previous business ventures. But throughout the development of *The Nutty Professor*, it created conflict. Grazer later accused Simmons of taking credit for a film he had barely worked on. When the film was released in 1996, Grazer even made sure Simmons was not invited to the premiere.

That same year, Simmons was an associate producer on another Abel Ferrara film, *The Funeral*. Starring Christopher Walken, Sean Penn, and Isabella Rossellini, *The Funeral* is about two brothers coping with the Mafia killing of their brother. The film received positive reviews for its complex explorations of morality and violence.

Simmons followed up *The Funeral* with two movies that had more obvious connections to hip-hop. He was executive producer for both *Gridlock'd* (1997) and *Def Jam's How to Be a Player* (1997). The former stars Tim Roth and Tupac Shakur (filmed in the year before the rapper's death). Janet Maslin of the *New York Times* described it as "a smart, well-made buddy film about two junkies desperate to kick the habit." The latter stars comedian Bill Bellamy, then host of *Def Comedy Jam*. Reviews of the film were mixed. Edward Guthmann of the *San Francisco Chronicle* called it "brainless." But Russell Smith of the *Austin* (Texas) *Chronicle* disagreed. "In its unpretentious way," Smith wrote, "this is really a surprisingly sharp little movie with plenty of irreverent insight for those who'll let it penetrate their PC [politically correct] defenses."

Simmons enjoyed his new role as film producer but never found the profits he made in other arenas. "Hollywood has yet to be good to me as a businessman," he noted in his autobiography.

The Second Golden Age

While Simmons had managed to achieve modest success in the film

IN FOCUS

dRush

Simmons added another new venture to his portfolio in 1999. He partnered with the advertising agency Deutsch to form the dRush agency. dRush marketed products to young consumers, ranging in age from eight to seventeen. Its first clients were Coca-Cola and HBO.

"We saw a need in the youth culture that wasn't being met," Donny Deutsch, chief executive of Deutsch, said. "Russell has his finger on the pulse of what's going on with young people, and we wanted to create a cutting edge agency." At first, the agency did more than $100 million in business, according to *Black Enterprise*. But dRush was not able to build on its early success the way Simmons and Deutsch had hoped. The joint venture dissolved after a couple years.

industry, Phat Farm continued to struggle. Finally, Simmons decided that he would begin running Phat Farm day to day.

Simmons decided the only way to rescue the company was to explore licensing again. Phat Farm signed licensing agreements with different companies to manufacture not just clothing but also bags, shoes, outerwear, watches, jewelry, and more.

Meanwhile, Simmons began slowly selling off Def Jam. He sold another 10 percent share of Def Jam to its major-label distributor, PolyGram. In 1998 PolyGram was acquired by Seagram, a Canadian beverage and entertainment conglomerate that already owned four record companies (Universal, MCA, Interscope, and Geffen). In purchasing PolyGram, Seagram took over five more: Mercury, Island, Motown, A&M, and Def Jam. Seagram renamed its combined music companies—which together formed the largest record company in the world—Universal Music Group.

With nine labels to contend with, Universal Music Group laid off many recording artists and employees. For Simmons the time had finally come to sell the label he had cofounded. In 1999 Seagram purchased the remaining 40 percent of Def Jam. Def Jam became part of a new division, Island Def Jam.

As part of the agreement, Simmons retained his role as chairman of Def Jam. He could have taken the money he made and started another record company. But he found it too difficult to leave behind his artists—who by then included Jay-Z, Method Man, and DMX.

For Simmons the late 1990s marked Def Jam's second golden age—even if the company was owned by someone else. "Though Def Jam in the '80s was a very special, groundbreaking label, it actually made more money and had bigger hits in the '90s," Simmons later recalled.

Family Life

The late 1990s marked a dramatic shift in Simmons's personal life as well as his professional life. Throughout his twenties, Simmons had seemingly changed girlfriends as often as he changed clothes. He slowed down in his mid-thirties, when he met Lee. After dating for years, Simmons and Lee decided to get married in December 1998.

They were first married in a civil ceremony. Then they had a more public wedding to celebrate their marriage with family and friends. Reverend Run (Joseph Simmons) presided over the wedding. Simmons reportedly wore Phat Farm casual wear and Adidas. Afterward, Simmons and Lee moved into a duplex penthouse loft in the Wall Street area, which they bought from rock guitarist Keith Richards for $2 million.

In 2000 the couple had their first child, a daughter named Ming Lee. "Until you have one [a baby], you don't really know what it's like," Simmons said. "Having a wife and a baby is a blessing that I wasn't even expecting." Two years later, the couple had a second daughter, Aoki Lee.

As his family grew, Simmons also discovered a more spiritual side. He had been taking yoga classes for several years. Yoga is a system of philosophy and movement that promotes a healthy body and mind. It emerged from the tradition of Hinduism. Simmons started taking the classes partly because the classes were filled with

Sibling bond: Russell and Kimora celebrate Russell's birthday in 2007 with their daughters Ming Lee *(left)* and Aoki Lee *(right)*.

USA TODAY Snapshots®

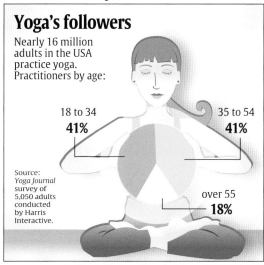

Yoga's followers

Nearly 16 million adults in the USA practice yoga. Practitioners by age:

18 to 34
41%

35 to 54
41%

over 55
18%

Source: *Yoga Journal* survey of 5,050 adults conducted by Harris Interactive.

By Michelle Healy and Veronica Salazar, USA TODAY, 2008

actresses and models. But gradually yoga came to be a spiritual anchor. "I first got addicted to the physical part of yoga," Simmons said. "When I began studying it, I realized that the physical part of it is just one of the eight steps. It's a beautiful practice. There are as many roads to God as there are people. Yoga is one of them."

Simmons's yoga practice led him to become a vegan. He also began meditating daily. Of all the rooms in his 35,000-square-foot (3,250 sq. m) mansion, Simmons's favorite was the meditation room.

Political Activism

As the new millennium began, Simmons became more politically active. He launched a short-lived website, 360hiphop.com, which covered hip-hop music, fashion, and culture with a political edge. 360 Hip Hop sponsored a Rap the Vote campaign (a variation on MTV's earlier campaign, Rock the Vote) to register young people to vote.

360 Hip Hop also helped sponsor two political marches in Washington, D.C. One urged Americans to "redeem the dream" of racial equality that Martin Luther King had spoken about in 1963. More than one hundred thousand marchers came to bring attention to issues such as police brutality and racial profiling.

In October 2000, Phat Farm and 360 Hip Hop also helped sponsor

Harmony: The Million Family March is seen from the Capitol in Washington, D.C., on October 16, 2000. Phat Farm sponsored the event that celebrated unity.

the Million Family March (named after the 1995 Million Man March led by Louis Farrakhan). The Million Family March celebrated family unity and promoted racial and religious harmony. Its organizers also encouraged marchers to work for public policies that benefited Americans of all races. The event included a historic speech by Farrakhan. Despite Farrakhan's previous antiwhite and anti-Semitic statements, this time he called for a less divisive approach to race and religion. Simmons had discussed the speech with Farrakhan just hours before he delivered it. "There is no question in my mind," Simmons wrote in his autobiography, "that the efforts made via the website and both marches helped stimulate an increased number of blacks to vote in November 2000."

Simmons took his political interests further in 2001. He founded a group called the Hip-Hop Summit Action Network. The group's leaders included rap stars, record company executives, and civil rights activists. Its wide agenda ran from the specific (lobbying against censorship in hip-hop) to the general (ending racism).

In forming the group, Simmons hoped to inspire young people to become more politically active and socially conscious. The network's nine-member board, chaired by Simmons, included Kweisi Mfume, president of the National Association for the Advancement of Colored People (NAACP), and Sean Combs. Most of the network's $200,000 yearly budget came from record companies, such as Sony and Universal. "Largely because of Mr. Simmons's visibility," wrote a *New York Times* reporter, "it is the first organization to receive national attention for exploring the nexus [link] between hip-hop and politics."

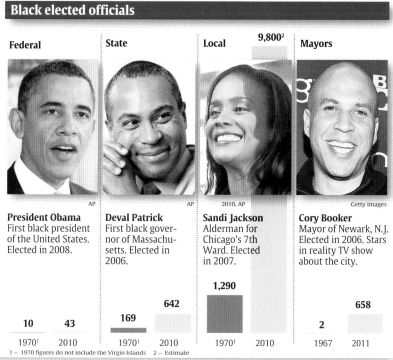

Black elected officials

Federal

President Obama
First black president of the United States. Elected in 2008.

AP

10	43
1970[1]	2010

State

Deval Patrick
First black governor of Massachusetts. Elected in 2006.

AP

169	642
1970[1]	2010

Local 9,800[2]

Sandi Jackson
Alderman for Chicago's 7th Ward. Elected in 2007.

2010, AP

1,290

1,290	
1970[1]	2010

Mayors

Cory Booker
Mayor of Newark, N.J. Elected in 2006. Stars in reality TV show about the city.

Getty Images

2	658
1967	2011

1 – 1970 figures do not include the Virgin Islands   2 – Estimate

Research by Melanie Eversley and Marisa Kendall; graphic by Julie Snider, USA TODAY, 2011

USA TODAY
Life
SECTION D
LIFE.USATODAY.COM

June 18, 2001

Rap summit aims to expand music's influence on society

From the Pages of
USA TODAY
Political, social and musical issues will be going to the top of the hip-hop community's agenda. Commitments were sealed to a variety of initiatives to be put into action immediately or in coming months as a result of the "Hip-Hop Summit: Taking Back Responsibility," which wrapped up last week. Here's a look at the focal points for action:

Politics. Lobbying efforts in Congress are planned to fight legislation aimed at restricting or censoring music, as well as attempts by the Federal Communications Commission to discourage radio stations from playing hip-hop by levying fines for offensive language. There also are plans to work with the Congressional Black Caucus to create more awareness about hip-hop among elected officials and to specifically support and oppose candidates at the ballot box.

As one of the community's first shows of strength, summit organizer Russell Simmons hopes to deliver his hip-hop constituency for Democrat Mark Green in the New York mayoral election this fall. "It's not just going to be about backing somebody," says hip-hop mogul Sean Combs. "It's going to be about political enlightenment, and (candidates) are going to have to live up to their responsibilities and show some accountability."

Marketing. In addition to accepting voluntary Recording Industry Association of America [RIAA] guidelines on parental advisory labels on explicit materials, it also was agreed that any Internet site promotions of CDs that carry warning labels would also be labeled.

"I thought what the participants did was a thoughtful way of making sure their rights to free speech were protected and that their responsibility to the community and parents was also respected," says Hilary Rosen of the RIAA. "I want people to know what they are getting," says Def Jam president Kevin Liles. "But I also want the consumer and parents to take the responsibility of knowing what you're buying."

Community: *(Left to right)* Canadian rapper Belly, TV personality Free, Russell Simmons, and singer Monica arrive at the third annual Hip-Hop Summit in 2007. The summit, held in Houston, Texas, was devoted to encouraging financial literacy among young African Americans and Latinos.

Social coalitions. Discussions began about coordinating the efforts of charities and organizations, such as linking Combs' literacy project, Daddy's House, with the Urban League, and Simmons' Rush Philanthropic Arts with the NAACP. Rappers and rap labels operate and support a broad range of charities that could reach even more people by tying in with older, broader-based social organizations. "One of the goals of the summit was to uplift the image of hip-hop," Simmons says. "You see many stories about rappers and their cars, but almost none about rappers and their charities."

Lyrics. A large number of participants agreed that it was their responsibility to continue to expand the topics covered by artists and ensure the authenticity of hip-hop's subject matter. Combs says that while rappers should rhyme about the things in their own environment, they should avoid making up songs about guns and violence simply to be exploitative.

—Steve Jones

Phat Farm Expands

During the late 1990s, Phat Farm grew to become the core business of Rush Communications. By the early 2000s, Simmons had expanded Phat Farm to include Baby Phat (a women's line overseen by Lee) and Phat Farm Kids. In 2001 Baby Phat alone grossed $30 million, and Phat Farm Kids grossed $25 million. Rush Communications grossed $192 million total that year. Just $17 million came from Simmons's other businesses. When he had first come up with the idea of an urban clothing line, "all the rappers laughed at me," Simmons recalled, "and now they all have their own lines coming out."

Runway family: Kimora Lee Simmons walks the runway with her daughters at a Baby Phat fashion show in 2004. Baby Phat was a women's fashion line under Phat Farm.

Def Poetry Jam

As Simmons worked to keep up with new trends in hip-hop, his brother Danny drew Russell's attention to live poetry readings. Readings by young poets had taken off in Danny's home of Manhattan. The poets would perform their poetry in front of crowds in theaters and nightclubs, sometimes improvising new poems onstage. Many members of this new crop of urban poets made guest appearances on rappers' albums as well. "These young poets come out of the same spirit as hip-hop," Simmons recalled, "but without music, they're challenged to say something . . . that stands on its own without a hot beat to back it up."

Danny suggested extending the Def Jam name to a show featuring these spoken-word performers. With Stan Lathan, the executive producer of *Def Comedy Jam*, Russell and Danny pitched a poetry series to HBO. Once again, HBO bit.

Russell Simmons Presents Def Poetry Jam first aired in 2001. Like *Def Comedy*, the new show found an enthusiastic audience. "If I'm in a high school in the ghetto right now," Simmons said, "and I ask, 'Who writes poetry?' eighty percent of the class raises their hands."

The show spawned a Broadway adaptation in 2002. *Russell Simmons Def Poetry Jam on Broadway* featured some of the most vivid performers from the HBO series. The diverse cast included young men and women of various races and sexual orientations, from cities across the country. The show was divided into four segments, each featuring a specific theme: identity, memories, love, and a final message.

Speaking out: Suheir Hammad *(left)*, Beau Sia *(center)*, and Georgia Me perform in *Russell Simmons' Def Poetry Jam on Broadway* in 2003. The play was adapted from the television show *Russell Simmons Presents Def Poetry Jam*.

December 14, 2001

Def Poetry brings artistic passion to TV

<u>From the Pages of</u>
<u>USA TODAY</u>

For a generation raised on the dazzle of high-tech music and video performances, poetry may seem a quaint, old-fashioned entertainment. But hip-hop impresario Russell Simmons doesn't think so, and he'll test that belief when poets speak their stuff on *Russell Simmons Presents Def Poetry*.

"The thing you're always selling in every melody, every film is heart. And poetry, when you're good at it, has the heart thing," says Simmons, who runs Def Jam Records and produced *Russell Simmons' Def Comedy Jam* for six years on HBO. Simmons says the bustling local and underground poetry scenes remind him of the state of urban comedy a few years ago, bubbling with creativity and ready for more mainstream exposure. And young audiences should relate, he says, because words and rhymes are so much a part of hip-hop entertainment. "Rap brought the spoken word back to people's minds," he says.

The four-episode series, hosted by rapper and actor Mos Def, features a mix of well-known poets; young, racially diverse performers; and a celebrity or two, including [singer] Jewel and [actor] Benjamin Bratt, who reads a poem by [playwright and poet] Miguel Pinero. Topics range from lighter matters to drugs and racial stereotypes.

"There's a conception of poetry as not being hip. We believe that it is hip," says Stan Lathan, who joins Simmons as executive producer. That means it "has to have some sort of meaning to the audience."

"If we can get a couple more cats like Russell to go against the grain, we can" have mainstream success, says Black Ice (Lamar Manson), who signed with Simmons' Def Jam label. The spoken-word artist from Philadelphia is working on a CD project. No matter what happens with the Def Jam deal, Black Ice will stick with his love: the spoken word. "You'll still catch me at the corner," he says.

—Bill Keveney

Unlike most Broadway productions, the show was deliberately under-rehearsed. It constantly changed based on the poets featured in each performance. When Jam Master Jay, the DJ from Run-D.M.C., was shot and killed just before the show opened in October 2002, two of the poets collaborated on a poem about his death. Poems in the show ranged from political to personal, humorous to serious, often in quick succession. In 2003 the show was awarded a Tony—the equivalent of an Oscar for live theater—in the category of Special Theatrical Event.

More Activism

In 2003 Simmons took his political activism to a new level, participating in two controversial campaigns. In February the Hip-Hop Summit Action Network called for a boycott of Pepsi products. The Pepsi company had canceled its advertising deal with the rapper Ludacris, who had come under fire for the obscene lyrics in his songs. But the company did not pull ads featuring rocker Ozzy Osbourne and his family, who used similar language on their reality TV show *The Osbournes.* Simmons called Pepsi on its double standard.

In the face of such a boycott, Pepsi officials quickly backed down. After negotiating with Simmons, Pepsi even agreed to donate $3 million to urban youth charities involved in the arts.

Simmons also volunteered to serve as a spokesperson for the controversial animal rights organization People for the Ethical Treatment of Animals (PETA). In August 2003, Simmons, wearing a PETA baseball cap, appeared in a full-page ad in the *Louisville Courier-Journal* newspaper. Louisville, Kentucky, is home to the fried chicken restaurant chain KFC. In the ad, Simmons called for a boycott of KFC until the company pledged to improve living conditions for the chickens it buys. Asked why Simmons was chosen to appear in the campaign, a PETA spokesperson said, "When Russell Simmons speaks, millions and millions of people listen."

In politics, as in business, Simmons quickly set about forming partnerships. The Hip-Hop Summit Action Network picked up the Rap

Hova: Jay-Z performs in Washington, D.C., while on tour during March 1999. Some civil rights activists criticized the music of Jay-Z and other Hip-Hop Summit artists.

the Vote campaign for the 2004 election, working with the NAACP. It also cosponsored a literacy drive with the Urban League. Both campaigns featured hip-hop artists as spokespeople.

Despite its worthy motives, the Hip-Hop Summit Action Network drew some criticism from more traditional civil rights activists. The group's stance against the censorship of hip-hop music—known for lyrics that attacked women and gays—undermined its credibility, these leaders claimed. "[Martin Luther] King died for 'Big Pimpin'?" one remarked, referring to a popular song by Jay-Z, who was involved in the group.

Simmons was unapologetic about hip-hop lyrics and about the group's links to the recording industry. He also claimed that he had no ambitions to run for political office, choosing to remain behind the scenes. "I don't want to run anything," he said. "I don't need power."

However, as he observed, "You can't avoid being political. You are part of a team. Your tax dollars. Your karma. If President [George W.] Bush goes to war with my tax dollars and I think it is an unjust war and I don't speak up, then I am not doing my job as a citizen."

IN F◯CUS

Too Candid?

In July 2004, Simmons had to testify in a court case involving Lyor Cohen. Simmons was not part of the lawsuit, but he was dragged into the case. Cohen was accused of understating the value of his share of Phat Fashions, the company that included Phat Farm and Baby Phat.

In his testimony, Simmons admitted many of the figures that he himself had given to reporters weren't accurate. For example, he had made an appearance on CNBC in which he claimed Phat Farm's sales for one year totaled $350 million. In fact, Phat Fashions' revenue for that time period came to just $14.3 million. The larger numbers "accurately reflected my optimism or my brand position statement," Simmons testified. "In other words, did I say it? I was hoping it would sound good. Maybe by that year the gross numbers were there. I don't know."

Asked whether he believed the numbers given about Phat Farm's revenue, Simmons said no. He also admitted "the amount of hype that goes on when I discuss the value of Phat Farm. It is how you develop an image for companies. So in other words, you give out false statements to mislead the public so they will then increase in their mind the value of your company." Later on in the testimony, Simmons asked, "It is not going to come out, right? About me lying to everybody? Right?" His testimony was made public around one year later.

Jeff Leeds wrote in the *New York Times* that "[Simmons's] testimony might be regarded as remarkably candid or remarkably troubling for any executive"—especially given his new roles as political activist and social commentator. Rush Communications later issued a statement claiming that Simmons had been preoccupied with a family matter and therefore had made "offhand and self-deprecating comments about his promotional activities."

Sale of Phat Farm

About this time, Simmons also began searching for a buyer for Phat Farm. He hoped to land a deal similar to his agreement at Def Jam—one that would leave him in charge and pay a substantial percentage of future profits. Simmons needed to sell Phat Farm so it could gain the resources of a larger company. Those resources—money, staff, and expertise—could help break Phat Farm into more department stores. "I just want growth for my company," Simmons said.

While searching for a buyer for Phat Farm, Simmons launched a new—and unlikely—partnership: UniRush. Simmons formed the group with Unifund, a company that buys uncollected debt from banks. Together, they offered consumers the RushCard. The card acts as a debit card, or prepaid credit card. After paying a $19.95 activation fee, users deposit funds into an account. Users then pay a small fee for each transaction to buy something or to get cash. The RushCard is an alternative to check-cashing agencies, which charge steep fees to cash the paychecks of people without checking accounts.

Fortune magazine pointed out that, as usual, Simmons's timing was good. Not only were debit cards becoming increasingly popular but the check-cashing industry was being criticized for taking advantage of the underprivileged.

The RushCard soon had detractors of its own. Some journalists criticized Unifund's practice of buying up bad debt. Others suggested that the fees charged to RushCard users meant it could be as damaging to users as check-cashing services. But by 2008, UniRush had issued more than 1.5 million cards.

In 2004 Simmons got the deal he wanted for Phat Farm. Kellwood Company bought Phat Farm for $140 million, retaining Simmons as chief executive of the division.

Rolling: Simmons rides through New York in 2007 in his new limousine, a Maybach 62.

Secrets of Success

■ ■ ■ ■ ■

In 2006 Simmons prepared for another intense life change. He filed for divorce from Kimora Lee after seven years of marriage. Simmons was forty-eight at the time, and she was thirty. In a statement to the media, he said that "Kimora and I will remain committed parents and caring friends with great love and admiration for each other. We will also continue to work side by side

Time with the girls: Russell shops with his daughters in January 2010 in California. Simmons has visitation with his daughters every eight weeks.

on a daily basis as partners in all of our businesses." Simmons has said elsewhere that he still considers Lee to be his best friend.

Although Simmons and Lee began to live separately, they continued to work together on the clothing lines they had developed—in the same building, in fact, with Lee working one floor above Simmons. Meanwhile, Simmons did not slow down in other areas. Following his experience with 360 Hip Hop, Simmons cocreated the hip-hop news and culture website Global Grind (globalgrind.com) in 2008. This second online effort was another success for Simmons.

Active and on Television

Entrepreneur magazine has labeled Simmons's ability to succeed at nearly everything he tries the "Russell Effect." Beginning in November 2010, television audiences were able to get an up-close look at the Russell Effect with the premiere of *Running Russell Simmons*. Simmons once again dove into unfamiliar territory, starring in his own reality television show on NBC's Oxygen network. *Running Russell Simmons* followed the work lives of Simmons, his executive assistant Simone Reyes, Global Grind copresident Tricia Clarke-Stone, and other Rush Communications staffers. Throughout the first season's six episodes, viewers saw the wide range of activities that make up Simmons's Life.

UniRush Under Fire

In the summer of 2011, criticisms of the UniRush RushCard turned to legal action. The Florida Attorney General's Office began to investigate UniRush for possibly making fraudulent claims and charging hidden fees. Some finance writers also stepped up their critiques of the RushCard. *Yahoo Finance* writer Farnoosh Torabi questioned whether the card was "really a long-term solution to establishing financial freedom," adding, "I think paying $9.95 a month just to store my money on a card is not necessarily the best option." Alexis Garrett Stodghill of the *Atlanta Post* accused the RushCard of being "a mediocre tool that exploits fear-based ignorance."

Simmons has remained defiant about the benefits of the RushCard for underprivileged consumers. In a 2011 interview with the *Forbes* website, Simmons called critics of the card "uneducated." The RushCard "was going to be just a philanthropic or social contribution," Simmons said, "but in order to make it work, we had to make it a business." He also argued that the card is "a much cheaper, better alternative to the banks."

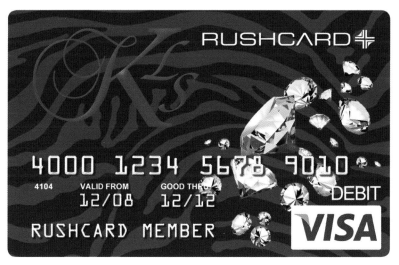

Financial freedom?: The Florida Attorney General's Office investigated the RushCard in 2011.

All in the family: Russell produced the television show *Run's House*, a reality show about his brother Reverend Run and his family. The family appeared on MTV's *TRL* in 2008 to promote the show. Reverend Run is pictured on the far right.

This includes meeting with art directors for a fund-raising event, butting heads with eccentric rock star Courtney Love, and visiting an animal park with his daughters.

In 2011 Simmons's business empire was still growing and changing. At the top was Rush Communications, which boasted numerous brands in entertainment, fashion, and finance. Among these brands was Def Jam Interactive, a software company responsible for video games such as *Def Jam Vendetta* and *Def Jam Rapstar*. Another, Simmons Lathan Media, produced television shows such as *Def Poetry Jam* and *Run's House*, a reality show starring Reverend Run and his family that ran from 2005 to 2009. Simmons continued to expand into fashion as well. The menswear brand American Classics, the sportswear brand Run Athletics, the jewelry brand Simmons Jewelry Co., and others show different sides of Simmons's stylistic vision.

USA TODAY

Life

SECTION D

LIFE.USATODAY.COM

August 29, 2001

Hip-hop artists unleash their clothing lines

From the Pages of USA TODAY   Platinum records aren't enough, it seems. Musicians are extending their style to other people's closets. An increasing number of recording artists are entering the fashion business or expanding their already established clothing lines.

In the past week, Sean "P. Diddy" Combs unveiled his underwear and lounge-wear collection, rapper Nelly announced plans to launch a line called VOKAL, Wu-Tang Clan's Wu-Wear Inc. added footwear to its clothing empire, R & B singer Sisqo unveiled his Dragon Collection, and Cash Money Millionaires launched Cash Money Clothing. Already available: Jay-Z's Rocawear, Busta Rhymes' Bushi Designs, Def Jam co-founder Russell Simmons' Phat Farm, Master P's No Limit Clothing (plus P Miller, his signature line), Fat Joe's FJ560, Naughty by Nature's Naughty Gear, and self-titled lines by Snoop Dogg, Ruff Ryders and Outkast.

Why threads? "It's a great opportunity to cross-market their brand identity," says Marshall Cohen, president of NPD, a market research company. "It's what I call a walking billboard. To be able to see an artist's name on a jacket, shirt or pair of pants is worth its weight in gold."

According to Cohen, urban wear is a $750 million business, and men's apparel makes up 68% of it. This year, Combs' 2-year-old Sean John line expects sales of $130 million. "Forty percent of our customers don't even know who Sean John is," says Jeffrey Tweedy, executive vice president of the line. "They just like the product."

Rocawear, targeted at males ages 14 to 30, offers men's clothes from $23 to $600 and kids' from $15 to $60. Sales for Rocawear, launched in 1999, are ahead of schedule and should reach $100 million this year with the addition of accessories such as belts and book bags. A women's line is next.

"It's been more about the clothes and the quality than the artist," says Rocawear CEO Damon Dash about the line's success. "People look at the clothes as being good clothes, as opposed to being Jay-Z's line. That might have gotten their curiosity going, but . . . you have to make quality clothes to stay in the business."

—Kelly Carter

A New Kind of Role Model

In the book *Hip-Hop Inc: Success Strategies of the Rap Moguls*, authors Richard Oliver and Tim Leffel analyzed Simmons's extraordinary track record. In business school, Oliver and Leffel wrote, students are taught that people are different and that therefore the products they buy must be different. But Simmons succeeded by taking the opposite tack. "He knew from the beginning, he knew from the street, he knew from understanding rather than judging people, that the gold was in the similarities not the

Accessories: Actor Nelson Ellis wears a necklace from Simmons Jewelry Co. in 2010.

differences," they wrote. "And he built his Empire of the 'Hood on that distinction."

Simmons also brings an extraordinary ability to recognize the next big thing, before anyone else is able to, Oliver pointed out. "He was the first to see that rap music was a lifestyle and could be translated into clothes, shoes, beverage, entertainment, design, watches, cars, and even financial services," Oliver wrote.

Although Simmons has recognized important trends time and again, he downplays his ability to see what others don't. "I don't pretend to discover something," Simmons once said. "By the time I get hold of something, it's already hot. I bring it to HBO, or Hollywood, or records, and it may be the first time that people have heard it outside of

In May 2009, United Nations secretary-general Ban Ki-moon appointed Russell Simmons the goodwill ambassador for the UN Slavery Memorial. The UN plans to build a memorial to educate people about the transatlantic slave trade and honor those who suffered because of it. Simmons works to raise awareness about the project.

the core, but these people are already cultural heroes in their community. What feels good to me is pretty commercial by the time I like it."

"If it weren't for Russell Simmons, I wouldn't be in the game," Sean Combs has said. "He created the blueprint for hip-hop.... He knows how to break down color barriers without compromising who he is. He never took off his Adidas or turned his hat."

According to Rod Kurtz of *Inc.* magazine, Simmons's influence was even broader. "Perhaps the most enduring

Two moguls: Russell Simmons honoring Sean Combs *(left)* at the Art for Life Gala in 2005. Combs credits Simmons for paving the way for the success of others.

IN F CUS

Overcoming Illness

In the summer of 2009, Russell Simmons faced a new challenge: a very serious infection called *Staphylococcus*, or *Staph*. *Staph* is a group of bacteria that can infect many different parts of the human body. Some *Staph* infections lead to grave illness or even death.

Simmons's infection started after he sought treatment for wrist pain he'd been feeling during yoga. His doctor gave Simmons two shots to treat swelling in the joints, using the same needle for both wrists—a mistake. Later that day, Simmons "awoke to the most intense physical pain [he'd] ever experienced." One wrist was extremely swollen. His doctor discovered that Simmons had contracted *Staph* through the needle.

Simmons quickly put together a medical team that could help him beat the infection. Despite his urgent need for treatment, Simmons later wrote that the experience provided him with a sense of calm and focus. "The little personal and professional anxieties that had ruled my life just a few days earlier were gone, eclipsed by my intense focus on [healing]," Simmons reflected. "I had been shocked into the present." This focus stayed with Simmons once he had overcome the illness. He claims to have pursued his many projects with a renewed sense of purpose after recovering.

legacy of Russell Simmons will be something he never set out to do," Kurtz noted. "Simmons has emerged as an entrepreneurial role model, providing guidance both directly and indirectly." Once again, Simmons was modest about his achievements. "All of the businesses I've gotten in," he joked, "I got in because I didn't know I couldn't."

Simmons's Advice

In his autobiography, Simmons offers several points of advice for aspiring entrepreneurs. One is that "in any new business, someone has to have a vision"—both an original insight and a plan for where the company should go. In the case of Def Jam, Simmons and Rubin understood that hip-hop was the new rock and roll and that it could have the same cultural—and financial—impact.

Another point is that "People aren't good or bad—just smart or stupid." Simmons gained fame for his ability to network. As he developed this skill, he was careful not to judge any person too quickly, and he worked to get along with all kinds of people. One final point is that "nothing happens the way it's supposed to." Simmons's favorite example of this is Phat Farm, which lost $10 million before becoming extremely profitable.

Although Simmons's network of businesses enjoys continued success, his focus has shifted more to politics, philanthropy, and sharing the knowledge he has gained. In 2007 he wrote the book *Do You! 12 Laws to Access the Power in You to Achieve Happiness and Success* with the help of author Chris Morrow. *Do You!* became a *New York Times* best seller.

Simmons cited an "old hip-hop expression" as the inspiration for the title. "'Do you!' . . . means do what you want to," he told one reporter. "Do what inspires you. Don't be a sheep." The book was originally titled *Russell Simmons's Laws of Success*. Fellow entrepreneur Oprah Winfrey suggested the change.

Do You! offers readers steps by which they can pursue their goals. Simmons based the steps on teachings he had learned through yoga. One chapter advises readers that "there are no failures, only quitters." Another urges them to "see [their] vision and stick with it."

"I'm not saying anything in this book that hasn't already been said before," Simmons admits in the book's introduction. "These are the same laws that Jesus Christ, Moses, Muhammad, Lord Buddha . . . and countless other inspirational people all shared." Yet the book is authentically Simmons, from its occasional profanity to its bluntness: "If you think there's a glass ceiling holding you back . . . shatter that glass, brush off the shards, and get on with your vision."

Author: Simmons signs copies of *Super Rich: A Guide to Having It All* during a book release party in January 2011.

In 2011 Simmons and Morrow published a follow-up book, *Super Rich: A Guide to Having It All.* Simmons dedicated it to his two daughters. Despite its title, *Super Rich* is not about achieving material wealth, but "something much greater." Simmons encourages readers to change their ways of thinking, so that "there's no difference between being broke and being a millionaire . . . you'll understand that you don't need money or toys to be happy." At the same time, Simmons argues, once you stop caring about financial rewards, they will begin to flow: "The road to enlightenment is paved with gold!"

TIMELINE

1957   Russell Simmons is born October 4 in Queens, New York.

1965   The Simmons family moves to Hollis, Queens.

1975   He enrolls in the City College of New York as a sociology major.

1977   Simmons decides to make a career in hip-hop. Two thousand people attend one of his parties at the Hotel Diplomat in New York City's Times Square.

1979   He coproduces the Kurtis Blow single, "Christmas Rappin'," the first hip-hop record released by a major label. He founds Rush Management, with Kurtis Blow as his first client.

1982   Rush Management opens its first office.

1983   Simmons coproduces "It's Like That" and "Sucker MC's" by his brother Joseph's rap group, Run-D.M.C.

1984   He cofounds record label Def Jam with Rick Rubin.

1985   Def Jam signs a distribution deal with major label Columbia. Simmons and Rubin buy a building for Def Jam's first office. Def Jam releases its first album, LL Cool J's *Radio*, which goes gold. The film *Krush Groove*, a fictionalized version of the Def Jam story, is released.

1988   *Tougher Than Leather*, a film featuring Run-D.M.C., is released. Rubin leaves Def Jam.

Partners: Rick Rubin *(left)* and Russell Simmons founded Def Jam in 1984. They are pictured here in 1988.

1988   Simmons takes sole control of the label.

1990   Simmons and Lyor Cohen launch Rush Associated Labels.

1992   *Def Comedy Jam* premieres on HBO.

1993   Simmons and Mark Beguda launch the fashion line Phat Farm.

1994   Simmons meets Kimora Lee, a seventeen-year-old fashion model. PolyGram buys a 50 percent stake in Def Jam.

1995   Simmons and his brothers cofound Rush Philanthropic Arts Foundation. *The Addiction*, a film Simmons produced, is released.

1996   *The Nutty Professor* and *The Funeral* are released.

1997   Simmons organizes a meeting that helps end the East Coast–West Coast hip-hop rivalry. *Gridlock'd* and Def Jam's *How to Be a Player* are released.

1998   He marries Lee.

1999   Simmons sells his remaining stake in Def Jam to Seagram. He and Donny Deutsch launch dRush, an advertising agency.

2000   He launches Baby Phat women's clothing and Phat Farm Kids. His first child, Ming Lee, is born.

2001   Simmons founds Hip-Hop Summit Action Network. *Russell Simmons Presents Def Poetry Jam* debuts on HBO.

2002   Simmons coproduces *Def Poetry Jam on Broadway*.

2003   *Def Poetry Jam* wins a Tony Award. Simmons's second child, Aoki Lee, is born. Simmons partners with Unifund to launch UniRush.

2004   He sells Phat Farm to Kellwood but remains CEO. He produces *Run's House*, a reality show, for MTV. He also testifies in a court case against Lyor Cohen.

2006   He files for divorce from Lee.

2008   He cocreates the hip-hop news and culture website GlobalGrind.com. He publishes *Do You! 12 Laws to Access the Power in You to Achieve Happiness and Success.*

Support: Russell Simmons participates in the New York City Occupy Wall Street protest against corruption and inequality on October 14, 2011.

2009   United Nations secretary-general Ban Ki-moon appoints Simmons the goodwill ambassador for the UN Slavery Memorial. Simmons survives a life-threatening *Staph* infection.

2011   Simmons publishes *Super Rich: A Guide to Having It All*. He also visits the Occupy Wall Street protest in New York City and on Twitter states his support for the protesters.

GLOSSARY

activism: organized efforts to bring about social or political change

anti-Semitic: expressing feelings or beliefs that are hostile to the Jewish faith or to Jewish people

civil ceremony: a nonreligious legal marriage

civil rights: the nonpolitical rights of a citizen, such as the right to equal treatment or personal liberty

disc jockey (DJ): a musician who uses record albums and a turntable to create new sounds

gangsta rap: a form of hip-hop that focuses on gang life. Gangsta rap originated in California during the late 1980s

hip-hop: a type of popular music that often features rapping along with background music created by a DJ

mainstream: a collection of dominant trends or something that is of a culture's dominant trends

philanthropy: charitable work or gifts

producer: the person who oversees the planning and financing of a television show, a movie, or a play or who oversees the recording of a song or an album

punk: a form of rock music that typically features loud guitars, shouted vocals, and fast tempos as well as simple song structures

rap: to deliver rhyming lyrics while accompanied by instrumental music

rhythm and blues (R & B): a traditionally African American form of popular music that features elements of jazz and blues

stand-up comedy: a form of comedy in which comedians deliver jokes or tell stories before a live audience

transatlantic slave trade: the practice of taking captives from Africa to North and South America to be sold for slave labor. The transatlantic slave trade was active from the 1500s until the 1800s.

turntable: a type of record player often used by hip-hop DJs

vegan: a person who consumes no meat or other animal-based food, including dairy products

yoga: a philosophy and set of movements that promote bodily control and well-being

SOURCE NOTES

4   Russell Simmons and Nelson George, *Life and Def: Sex, Drugs, Money and God* (New York: Crown Publishers, 2001), 187.

5   Ibid., 184.

6   Ibid., 220.

7   Meg Cox, "If a Big Beat Zaps You Out of a Nap, the Music Is Rap," *Wall Street Journal*, December 4, 1984.

8   Jeff Stark, "Brilliant Careers: Russell Simmons," *Salon*, July 6, 1999, http://www.salon.com/people/bc/1999/07/06/simmons/index.html (May 14, 2011).

8   Simmons and George, *Life and Def*, 4.

8   Christopher Vaughn, "Russell Simmons' Rush for Profits," *Black Enterprise*, December 1992, 69.

12   Simmons and George, *Life and Def*, 12.

14   Ibid., 19.

16   *Journeys in Black: Russell Simmons*. DVD (Studio City, CA: Black Entertainment Television, 2003).

16   Simmons and George, *Life and Def*, 23.

18   Ibid.

18   *Journeys in Black*.

21   Simmons and George, *Life and Def*, 32.

21   Ibid., 34.

22   *Journeys in Black*.

24   Simmons and George, *Life and Def*, 35.

26   Ibid., 36.

28–29   Rod Kurtz, "Russell Simmons, Rush Communications," *Inc.*, April 2004.

29   Simmons and George, *Life and Def*, 74.

32   Ibid., 65.

33   *Journeys in Black*.

35   Simmons and George, *Life and Def*, 99.

35   Ibid., 77.

35   Stacy Gueraseva, *Def Jam, Inc.: Russell Simmons, Rick Rubin and the Extraordinary Story of the World's Most Influenctial Hip-Hop Label* (New York: One World, 2005), 30.

38   *Journeys in Black*.

38   Simmons and George, *Life and Def*, 84.

40   Gueraseva, *Def Jam, Inc.*, 53.

40   Ibid., 62.

41   Simmons and George, *Life and Def*, 84.

41   Ibid., 79.

43   Gueraseva, *Def Jam, Inc.*, 50.

44   *Journeys in Black.*

44   Simmons and George, *Life and Def*, 99.

44   Ibid., 85.

45   Ibid.

45   Stephen Holden, "A Young Company Leads Rap Music into the Mainstream," *New York Times*, August 11, 1987.

47   Gueraseva, *Def Jam, Inc.*, 140.

48   Ibid., 138.

49   Richard Harrington, "Tougher Than Leather," *Washington Post*, September 17, 1988.

49   Simmons and George, *Life and Def*, 102.

49–50 Gueraseva, *Def Jam, Inc.*, 151.

50   Simmons and George, *Life and Def*, 109.

50   Gueraseva, *Def Jam, Inc.*, 153.

51   Simmons and George, *Life and Def*, 109.

51   Ibid., 179.

52   Ibid., 111.

52   Gueraseva, *Def Jam, Inc.*, 244.

53   Simmons and George, *Life and Def*, 180.

55–56 Vaughn, "Russell Simmons' Rush for Profits," 72.

56   Gueraseva, *Def Jam, Inc.* 180.

57   Vaughn, "Russell Simmons' Rush for Profits," 72.

57   Simmons and George, *Life and Def*, 137.

59   Ibid., 125.

60   Vaughn, "Russell Simmons' Rush for Profits," 72.

60   Jonathan Hicks, "A Big Bet for the Godfather of Rap," *New York Times*, June 14, 1992.

60–61 Simmons and George, *Life and Def*, 128.

63   Ibid., 155.

63   Julie Salamon, "Turning the Tables, the Establishment Takes on Hip-Hop," *New York Times*, September 6, 2000.

63   *Black Enterprise*, December 1992, cover.

63   Gueraseva, *Def Jam, Inc.*, 243.

64   Ian Fisher, "Phat City," *New York Times*, April 4, 1993.

64   Ibid.

64   Simmons and George, *Life and Def*, 157.

64   Ibid., 158.

65   Ibid.

65   Simmons and George, *Life and Def*, 115.

66   Kevin Chappell, "The Half-Billion-Dollar Hip-Hop Empire of Russell Simmons," *Ebony*, July 2003, 172.

66   Ibid.

66–67   Simmons and George, *Life and Def*, 195.

68   Ibid., 178.

68   Ibid., 113.

68   Gueraseva, *Def Jam, Inc.*, 243.

69   Simmons and George, *Life and Def*, 120.

70   Ibid., 143.

72   Janet Maslin, "Gridlock'd," *New York Times*, January 29, 1997, http://www.nytimes.com/library/film/gridlock-film-review.html (May 14, 2011).

72   Edward Guthmann, "How to Be a Player," *San Francisco Chronicle*, August 9, 1997.

72   Russell Smith, "Def Jam's How to Be a Player," *Austin Chronicle*, August 15, 1997.

72   Simmons and George, *Life and Def*, 120.

72   Stuart Elliott, "Deutsch Hopes to Reach Young Consumers Better by Forming a Venture with Rush Communications," *New York Times*, November 19, 1999.

73   Simmons and George, *Life and Def*, 194.

74   *Journeys in Black*.

75   Ibid.

76   Simmons and George, *Life and Def*, 174.

77   Felicia R. Lee, "Hip-Hop Is Enlisted in Social Causes," *New York Times*, June 22, 2002.

80   Richard W. Oliver and Tim Leffel, *Hip-Hop Inc: Success Strategies of the Rap Moguls* (New York: Thunder's Mouth Press, 2006), 77.

80–81   Simmons, *Life and Def*, 226.

81   Jon Pareles, "A New Platform for the New Poets," *New York Times*,

November 10, 2002.

83 Sherri Day, "Another Celebrity Takes on KFC over the Treatment of Animals," *New York Times*, August 21, 2003.

84 Ibid.

84 Ibid.

84 Julie Schlosser, "Russell Simmons Wants You—to Vote," *Fortune*, May 17, 2004, http://money.cnn.com/magazines/fortune/fortune_archive/2004/05/17/369608/index.htm (May 14, 2011).

86 Tracie Rozhon, "Can Urban Fashion Be Def in Des Moines?" *New York Times*, August 24, 2003.

85 Jeff Leeds, "Don't Believe the Hype. A Hip-Hop Mogul Says It's Propaganda," *New York Times*, May 16, 2005.

85 Ibid.

85 Ibid.

85 Ibid.

85 Ibid.

85 Ibid.

87–88 Stephen M. Silverman and Tiffany McGee, "Russell, Kimora Lee Simmons Split," *People*, March 31, 2006, http://www.people.com/people/article/0,,1178541,00.html (May 14, 2011).

88 Ibid.

89 Farnoosh Torabi "Russell Simmons' RushCard: Not the Best Deal for Consumers," *Yahoo! Finance*, March 22, 2011, http://finance.yahoo.com/banking-budgeting/article/112403/russell-simmons-rushcard-not-best-deal?mod=bb-creditcards (July 11, 2011).

89 Alexis Garrett Stodghill "Russell Simmons' RushCard Under Investigation for Hidden Fees," *Atlanta Post*, June 20, 2011, http://atlantapost.com/2011/06/20/russell-simmons-rush-card-under-investigation-for-hidden-fees/ (July 11, 2011).

89 Zach O'Malley Greenburg "Russell Simmons Defends the Rush Card," *Forbes*, March 18, 2011, http://blogs.forbes.com/zackomalleygreenburg/2011/03/18/russell-simmons-defends-the-rush-card/ (July 11, 2011).

92 Jeff Leeds, "Don't Believe the Hype. A Hip-Hop Mogul Says It's Propaganda," *New York Times*, May 16, 2005.

92 Ibid.

92–93 Pareles, "A New Platform."

93 Chappell, "The Half-Billion-Dollar Hip-Hop Empire," 178.

93–94 Kurtz, "Russell Simmons, Rush Communications."

94 Ibid.

94 Simmons and Morrow, *Super Rich: A Guide to Having It All*.

94 Ibid.

94–95 Simmons, *Life and Def*, 221.

95 Ibid., 222.

95 Ibid., 223.

95 Deborah Solomon "Questions for Russell Simmons: Hip-Hop Guru," *New York Times*, April 29, 2007.

95 Russell Simmons and Chris Morrow, *Do You! 12 Laws to Access the Power in You to Achieve Happiness and Success* (New York: Gotham Books, 2007), 4.

95 Ibid.

96 Russell Simmons and Chris Morrow, *Super Rich: A Guide to Having It All*. New York: Gotham Press, 2011, http://books.google.com/books?id=-S77HojSVc0C <http://books.google.com/books?id=-S77HojSVc0C> (November 4, 2011).

96 Ibid.

96 Ibid.

SELECTED BIBLIOGRAPHY

Chappell, Kevin. "The Half-Billion-Dollar Hip-Hop Empire of Russell Simmons." *Ebony*, July 2003, 168–169, 172, 174, 178.

Charnas, Dan. *The Big Payback: The History of the Business of Hip-Hop*. New York: New American Library, 2010.

Gueraseva, Stacy. *Def Jam, Inc.: Russell Simmons, Rick Rubin, and the Extraordinary Story of the World's Most Influential Hip-Hop Label*. New York: One World, 2005.

Journeys in Black: Russell Simmons. DVD. Studio City, CA: Black Entertainment Television, 2003.

Krush Groove. DVD. Burbank, CA: Warner Home Video, 2003. First released 1985.

Oliver, Richard W., and Tim Leffel. *Hip-Hop Inc.: Success Strategies of the Rap Moguls*. New York: Thunder's Mouth Press, 2006.

Simmons, Russell with Chris Marrow. *Super Rich: A Guide to Having It All*. New York: Gotham Books, 2011.

Simmons, Russell, and Nelson George. *Life and Def: Sex, Drugs, Money and God*. New York: Crown Publishers, 2001.

Vaughn, Christopher. "Russell Simmons' Rush for Profits." *Black Enterprise*, December 1992, 66–74.

FURTHER READING AND WEBSITES

All Music
> http://allmusic.com
> This online music resource allows you to look up album reviews, artist biographies, and more. The site includes a biography of Russell Simmons as well as a list of his projects.

Brill, Marlene Targ. *America in the 1990s*. Minneapolis: Twenty-First Century Books, 2010.

Brill, Marlene Targ. *America in the 1980s*. Minneapolis: Twenty-First Century Books, 2010.

Chang, Jeff. *Can't Stop, Won't Stop: A History of the Hip-Hop Generation*. New York: St. Martin's Press, 2005.

Def Jam Recordings: The First 25 Years of the Last Great Record Label. New York: Rissoli, 2011.

Doeden, Matt. *Will Smith: Box Office Superstar*. Minneapolis: Twenty-First Century Books, 2009.

Donovan, Sandy. *The African American Experience*. Minneapolis: Twenty-First Century Books, 2010.

Golus, Carrie. *Tupac Shakur: Hip-Hop Idol*. Minneapolis: Twenty-First Century Books, 2010.

Hip-Hop Summit Action Network
> http://www.hsan.org
> The Hip-Hop Summit Action Network's official site features videos, articles, and a calendar of upcoming events related to national and community activism.

Medina, Tony, and Louis Reyes Rivera, eds. *Bum Rush the Page: A Def Poetry Jam*. New York: Three Rivers Press, 2001.

People for the Ethical Treatment of Animals: The Animal Rights Organization
> http://www.peta.org
> Learn more about PETA, an animal rights group for which Russell Simmons has served as a spokesperson.

Purperheart, Helen. *Yoga Exercises for Teens: Developing a Calmer Mind and a Stronger Body*. Alameda, CA: Hunter House Publishing, 2009.

Rankin, Kenrya. *Start It Up: The Complete Teen Business Guide to Turning Your Passions into Pay*. San Francisco: Zest Books, 2011.

Rosenthal, Beth, ed. *Should Music Lyrics Be Censored?* Detroit: Greenhaven Press, 2011.

Rush Communications
http://www.rushcommunications.com
This site has more information about Russell Simmons's many different companies, including Def Jam Interactive and UniRush.

Rush Philanthropic Arts Foundation
http://www.rushphilanthropic.org
Rush Philanthropic Arts Foundation sponsors art programs for urban youths and helps artists of color share their work with the world.

Russell Simmons (UncleRUSH) on Twitter
http://twitter.com/#!/unclerush
Check out advice and life updates from Russell Simmons on the social networking site Twitter.

The Victims of Slavery and the Transatlantic Slave Trade Memorial
http://www.unslaverymemorial.org
This site outlines the United Nations' transatlantic slave trade memorial project and provides a history of the slave trade.

INDEX

PHOTO ACKNOWLEDGMENTS

The images in this book are used with the permission of: © Todd Plitt/USA TODAY, pp. 1, 3, 9, 32, 36, 54, 61, 78, 82, 87, 91; © Michael Grecco/Hulton Archive/Getty Images, p. 4; © Steve Granitz Archive/WireImage/Getty Images, p. 5 (left); © Ron Galella, Ltd./WireImage/Getty Images, pp. 5 (right), 39, 59; © Tim Dillon/USA TODAY, pp. 6, 76; © Mike Guastella/WireImage/Getty Images, p. 7; Library of Congress, pp. 10 (HAER NY,31-NEYO,160-5), 13 (LC-DIG-ppmsca-03128); © Jerritt Clark/Getty Images, p. 12; © Frederic Lewis/Hulton Archive/Archive Photos/Getty Images, p. 17; © Robert Hanashiro/USA TODAY, p. 19 (top); © Echoes/Redferns/Getty Images, p. 19 (middle); © Michael Ochs Archives/Getty Images, pp. 19 (bottom), 31, 56; © Barry Winiker/Photolibrary/Getty Images, p. 20; © Soul Brother/FilmMagic/Getty Images, p. 22; © Stephen Wright/Redferns/Getty Images, p. 23; © David Corio/Michael Ochs Archives/Getty Images, pp. 25, 57; © Al Pereira/Michael Ochs Archives/Getty Images, p. 27; © Waring Abbott/Michael Ochs Archives/Getty Images, p. 29; © Ed Molinari/ NY Daily News Archive via Getty Images, p. 34; © Lisa Haun/Michael Ochs Archives/ Getty Images, p. 37; © Fotos International/Archive Photos/Getty Images, p. 38; © Pace Gregory/CORBIS SYGMA, p. 42; © Crystalite Productions/The Kobal Collection/Art Resource, NY, p. 43; © Suzie Gibbons/Redferns/Getty Images, p. 45; © Joyce Ravid/ CORBIS, p. 46; © Photofest, p. 49; © Dimitrios Kambouris/VF11/WireImage/Getty Images, p. 51; © USA TODAY, p. 53; © Columbia/The Kobal Collection/Art Resource, NY, p. 55; © Anthony Barboza/Archive Photos/Getty Images, p. 58; © Jeff Kravitz/ FilmMagic/Getty Images, p. 60; © Frank Micelotta/Getty Images, p. 62; © Henry McGee/Globe Photos/ZUMA Press, p. 66; © James Leynse/CORBIS, p. 69; © Alexander Tamargo/Getty Images, p. 70; © Universal/Bruce McBroom/The Kobal Collection/Art Resource, NY, p. 71; © Johnny Nunez/WireImage/Getty Images, pp. 74, 93; © Eileen Blass/USA TODAY, p. 79; © Carlo Allegri/Getty Images, p. 80; AP Photo/Robert Spencer, p. 81; © Rick Williams/USA TODAY, p. 84; © BuzzFoto/FilmMagic/Getty Images, p. 88; PRNewsFoto/UniRush LLC/AP Photo, p. 89; © Bryan Bedder/Getty Images, p. 90; © Matthew Simmons/Getty Images, p. 92; © Kris Connor/Getty Images, p. 96; © Ebet Roberts/Redferns/Getty Images, p. 97; AP Photo/Mary Altaffer, p. 99.

Front cover: © Alberto E. Rodriguez/Getty Images.
Back cover: © Eileen Blass/USA TODAY

Main body text set in USA TODAY Roman Regular 10.5/15.

ABOUT THE AUTHOR

Carrie Golus holds a BA and an MA in English from the University of Chicago. Her previous titles for Lerner Publishing Group include the star-reviewed *Tupac Shakur* Lifeline biography. She lives in Chicago with her twin sons.